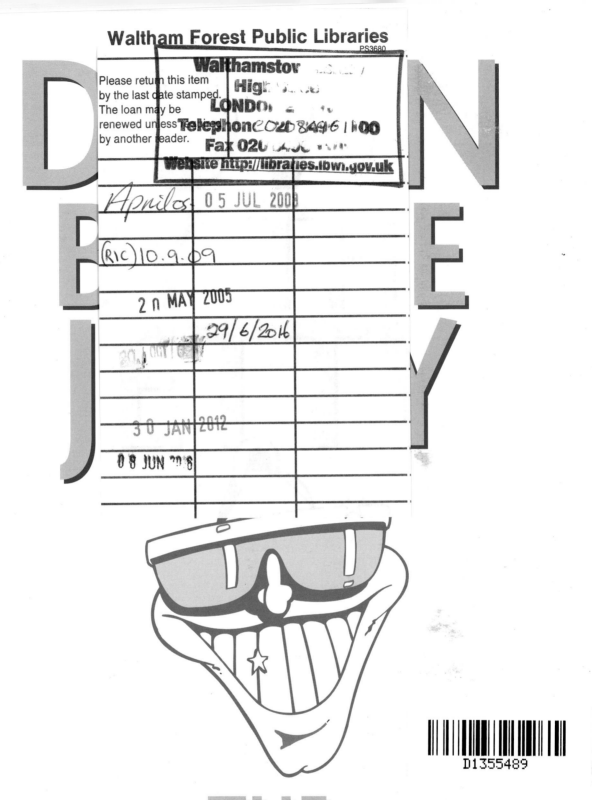

D1355489

THE
DR FEELGOOD
STORY

TONY MOON

Revised Edition Published in 2002 by
NORTHDOWN PUBLISHING LIMITED
PO Box 49, Bordon
Hants GU35 0AF

British Library Cataloguing-in-Publication Data
A catalogue for this book is available from the British Library

ISBN 1-900711-15

Printed in the UK
Title first published 1997
Cover art: Vince Ray (www.vince-ray.com)

PICTURE CREDITS
Photographs in this book have been reproduced courtesy of the Dr Feelgood/ Grand Records archives. Thanks are also due to: Wilko Johnson, Andrew Lauder, Wendy Wisbey Agency, Frans Moerland, Decca Record Company/Roger Dopson, Demon Records, Atlantic Records, Liberty/United Artists Records, Joe Petagno, Hugo Williams, Chalkie Davies/*NME*, Roy Carr, Gail Mezey, Annette de Jong, Trevor Rogers, Andrew Crowley, DJ Smith, Jane N Hill, Ari-Veikko Peltonen, Snappy, Leigh Times Group, Keith Morris, Bob Bromide, Mike Tighe, James Cumpsty, Pete Middlebrough.
While every effort has been made to trace the owners of photographs used, this has sometimes proved impossible: such copyright owners are invited to contact the publishers.

The publishers also gratefully acknowledge discographical assistance from Chris Frances and Yair Goodfellow.

www.northdown.demon.co.uk

Opposite: Boswell and Johnson. The author (right) keeps (Feel)good company.

CONTENTS

ACKNOWLEDGEMENTS

Whenever undertaking a project such as writing a book or making a documentary film, one often sets about it with a feeling of apprehension. For to get to the heart of the matter an intensive period of research must first be undertaken. Usually this process reveals things that you had not anticipated or even imagined. Dark stuff that shatters a naive first impression. I can only say that in researching and writing this book about Dr Feelgood the opposite was to prove to be true.

I should like to thank the following without whose interest and assistance I could not have done without:

Wilko Johnson, the Big Figure, John B Sparks, Gypie Mayo, Johnny Guitar, Gordon Russell, Nick Lowe, Jake Riviera, Andrew Lauder, Larry Wallis, Nigel Kerr, Will Birch, Mike Vernon, Dave Bronze, Dai Davies, John Eichler, Dean Kennedy, Brian Pearson, Pete Gage and especially the present members of Dr Feelgood – Kevin Morris, Steve Walwyn, Phil Mitchell and Robert Kane.

Special thanks go to Michael Heatley for asking in the first place. Sharon Hood for persevering. And Ann Adley in the office for additional info.

Above all I would like to thank Chris Fenwick for his remarkable candour and for letting me get close.

This book is dedicated to the memory of Lee Brilleaux 1952-1994. May the road rise with you.

Tony Moon

FOREWORD

There's been good times and bad times, but what the hell? For an
R&B outfit to still keep them rockin' in the aisles after 30 years,
there must be something there – and that something comes from
you, the audience.

A blinding Dr Feelgood show is a two-way affair. It's not just one
bunch of barmpots entertaining another, it's about a special
connection between the band and the crowd, a soul-mate feeling
which creates the unique 'Feelgood' vibe. It's about the thumping
warm glow deep in your chest, it's about hearing the opening chords
to your favourite song and the hairs on the back of your neck
standing to attention, it's about the pint in your hand splashing about
when you spontaneously gyrate.

It's your enjoyment, your enthusiasm and your support that keeps us
out there on the road, and as long as we have that we'll keep on
doing it – without it there would be no story.

Here's to each and every one of you.

Cheers

Chris Fenwick

THE GREATEST LOCAL BAND IN THE WORLD

S ometime in 1972, in the bleak cul-de-sac of England that is Canvey Island, Essex, four distinctly unlovable-looking moptops came together and fashioned something wild and totally unpredictable out of their various enthusiasms for rock'n'roll, R&B and straight blues music.

Having jump-started the hybrid creature they'd created with the opening riff from a Bo Diddley tune fused with the guttural wheeze of a beer-soaked harmonica, the beast grew progressively bigger. Eventually – and inevitably – it was soon to outgrow the depressing confines of its birthplace and embark upon a wrecking tour that was to take it, in time, all around the world. That 'thing' was the band we know as Dr Feelgood.

By the time they first hit the beer-stained stages of the rough and ready London pub circuit in 1973, the Feelgoods were clearly a breed apart – a stripped-down, all-walking and talking anachronism. The sweat-stained clothes they stood up in soon became a frayed anti-fashion statement of intent, in sharp contrast to the more popular apparel favoured by most rock'n'rollers at the time – the flared satin loon pant and the stack-heeled boot. In short, Dr Feelgood were the band to give rock the wake-up call it urgently needed.

Once they'd got into their stride, both on stage and on record, the Feelgoods set about beating on every long-haired and woolly-thinking head in the country and didn't stop until all had surrendered to their distinctive short-back-and-sides, no-nonsense ethic. This campaign of attrition reached its peak in 1976 when 'Stupidity', the crisp and definitive recording of their live act, was sent to Number 1 in the UK LP chart by the record-buying public. Maybe nobody knew it at the time, but this was the first iceberg of many to come which, over the next few years, was to rip a hole through the hull of the increasingly complacent British music industry. Waiting on the horizon were others...but Dr Feelgood did it first.

The earliest Feelgood line-up on location in Canvey featured, from the left, guitarist Wilko Johnson, bassist John B Sparkes, vocalist Lee Brilleaux and drummer John Martin, aka the Big Figure.

'Anyone wonder where the emotion has gone out of music?'
Local Paper Ad

'Where are all the characters and the great rock'n'roll music I grew up with ?'
Alan McGee (Founder of Creation Records)

For those inveterate rock'n'rollers among us, 'the past', as Captain Beefheart would one day remind us, 'sure is tense.' Those of us of a certain age, mmm; perhaps vintage is a more distinguished descriptor? Whatever… Those of us who can recall rock'n'roll before it became something of a career move for corporate shills with nothing more urgent on their idiot minds than to be famous will surely empathise with the above quotes.

Of late, it seems as if rock'n'roll has somehow taken the king's shilling and flattened out. Somewhere between that advert for jeans and another for an underarm deodorant the urgency has abated. The revolt into style has been concluded. One rock'n'roll commentator recently asserted that 'Life is too short for joke bands.' All too true. Authentic heroes in the mould of a Dury, a (Rory) Gallagher and, of course, a Brilleaux seem, in these cynical times, a little thin on the ground.

Snap back to the Southend Kursal in '76. On stage Dr Feelgood are going through their paces

and ritually tearing the place apart. There is Wilko, John B Sparks and Big Figure and of course resplendent in a filthy white suit stained to perfection with a cocktail of lager and sweat and more lager – singer, front man, nutter Lee Brilleaux barking into the mic like an uninivited wedding guest from hell.

The thing of it is that us lot who were right down there in the pit, right in the belly of the beast – caught in the glare of the white light which emanated from behind the drum riser – with our arms held up in the air in a dual act of submission and communion during the tour de force that was 'Riot in Cell Block No 9' are now the people we never thought we'd be. Dads, uncles, godfathers, pot-bellied blokes, divorced, bald geezers with mortgages to pay, lawns to mow, the whole bit.

In attics all over the UK is the evidence of the crime. Cardboard boxes packed with 12-inch vinyl memories of this magical past. Check out my own copy of 'Down By The Jetty', still in its clear plastic protective sleeve. On the back in expansive flowing biro: 'To Tony, from Lee Brilleaux and Sparko.' Fucking hell.

In my fanzine I once famously (to some) hurriedly scribbled three guitar box chords onto a page and added the urgent slogan 'Now Form a Band.' The impetus for that simple cri de coeur was always Dr Feelgood, whose rough and ready antics had already caught the imaginations of most

Up against the wall – the Feelgoods' 1997 line-up. Left to right: Steve Walwyn (guitar), Pete Gage (vocals), Kevin Morris (drums) and Phil Mitchell (bass).

adolescent youths across England in the mid seventies. The reason? Loads of them, really, but primarily the Feelgoods came over like they were mates who liked each other and who had actually gotten together for a bit of a lark. Everything else was a bonus.

These days, being in a band is often akin to a corporate career move. One critic described the output from a lot of so-called 'top acts' of today as being little more than 'Tupperware rock'. The Sultan of Seed, Tom Waits, hit the nail on the head when he wondered why such dullards don't just quit the pretence – put on a suit and tie and turn up at Coca-Cola (or whatever corporation they are hawking), get themselves a desk and a phone and really go to work.

Thanks to their mission to play blues music as long as people want to hear it, Dr Feelgood has emerged over the years as a great British institution, a proving ground for some of the finest English R&B players in the country. Some people, like writer, musician and long-time friend of the band Will Birch, put it more strongly. He asserts that Dr Feelgood were, in the post-1960s Beatles and Stones world, 'the most influential group of the past 25 years' simply because 'they caused more things to happen than anyone else.'

One way they achieved this was because of the total commitment of Lee Brilleaux to the live arena. Birch again: 'He inspired a new generation of British rock'n'rollers who went on to keep exciting live rock'n'roll going and that has had a resounding effect around the world.

'He made it not a sin to get up on stage and entertain. First and foremost he was an entertainer and he gave the function of entertaining a new value which had, by the early 1970s, become lost. Everyone then took themselves incredibly seriously. Everyone was deep and introverted and he made it plausible and real again to get up on a stage, take the audience by the scruff of the neck and entertain – that's his legacy.'

As well as being the definitive British R&B group, Dr Feelgood are also rightly regarded as being the 'godfathers of punk'. A handy journalistic soundbite, perhaps, but nevertheless the

Feelgoods were the ones who came forward to dispense much-needed spiritual guidance when all around was dark and very flared. For before the glorious punk campaigns of the late 1970s, when all the great rock icons of the previous decade were set upon and dismantled like old steam engines after electrification, stood the Feelgoods in all their tatty-suited glory.

Their debut album, 'Down By The Jetty', had been recorded in impossibly unfashionable mono and packaged in a great 1960s-looking retrospective sleeve which featured the band posing on the cover and looking like they were genuinely pissed off about something or other. This was the punk attitude made flesh when the spotty lads from the Sex Pistols were still in short trousers.

A confused American writer delivered a backhanded compliment when he summed up the Feelgood sound by saying that '…they sound like a sparse backing band for a lead singer who never appears.' Yet this cheap jibe does hint in a perverse way at the bare-boned, stripped-down sound the band put over – and at the same time manages to ignore the fist-punching menace that was Lee Brilleaux in full flight. He was the bank clerk from hell who liked to say 'No', his aggressive mic-grabbing technique having once been likened to 'an eagle swooping down on its prey.'

But let's not forget bug-eyed psycho-killer guitarist and songwriter Wilko Johnson, whose band this was as well. He'd based his own unique 'two for one' lead/rhythm style on his hero – Mick Green of the legendary Johnny Kidd and the Pirates.

Without Wilko's overtly theatrical presentation, playing the fool to Brilleaux's leering king, combined with his mastery of 'Johnny B Goode' guitar licks and the innate ability to actually write an authentic-sounding song in a genuine urban

blues idiom, Dr Feelgood would have probably never left Canvey Island.

Together, Brilleaux and Johnson were the public face of this perverse little musical unit. Backing this vaudeville-like duo and completing the original line-up was John B Sparkes on bass and John 'Big Figure' Martin on drums – two smash-and-grab rhythm merchants who together could lay down a bog-standard backbeat and make it sound like it had never been played before. This clenched fist of rhythm was the backdrop against which Brilleaux and Johnson exhibited their crazed and often demented magic.

It was around this time that my mate and I started to follow the Feelgoods. The image that Lee Brilleaux evoked as a frontman became, for us, a barometer against which anything and everything could be measured and tested. For example, if we were watching something on the telly, listening to something new or being asked to consider some new concept our immediate retort would be… 'yes, but would Brilleaux like it?'

For example, would Brilleaux like gatefold double album sleeves? Would Lee Brilleaux like BBC2? Would Brilleaux like croissants for breakfast? Would Brilleaux smoke low-tar tipped cigarettes? Would Brilleaux enjoy *The South Bank Show*? Would Brilleaux use chopsticks instead of a knife and fork? Would Brilleaux wear that style of

shirt? The answer to these and a hundred other lifestyle questions always seemed to be a very positive and always life-affirming NO HE FUCKIN' WOULDN'T.

Since researching and writing this book I've discovered that this was a thought process which friends of Lee's such as Nick Lowe and Larry Wallis also used to experience: Brilleaux, you see, had that type of magnetism.

At the heart of this obsession was the notion of pilgrimage – and that naturally involved regular trips to the home of the Feelgoods. My mate and I would often jump in his van and head down the A13, the depressing umbilical cord linking Essex with the rest of Britain, to Canvey Island – in reality little more than an Oil Terminal with a few houses chucked around it. Its very geographical location seemed to cry out for an accompanying

soundtrack of bare-boned beat music with no frills, no colour, no overdubs. As Lee himself said 'You're not exactly inspired by the place to sing about things to do with beauty, are you?'

After pilgrimage came the need for personal audience with our chosen idols. The means to achieve this came about when we started our own fanzine. One night at the Nashville Rooms in West Kensington we spotted Lee propping up the bar. We sheepishly went over and asked him for an interview – and, to our utter amazement, he agreed on the spot. 'Meet you at Stiff Records on Tuesday.' On these memorable occasions, of which there were several, Brilleaux revealed himself to be a perceptive and canny operator who was willing to go out of his way to accommodate even the likes of us with our badly-typed, semi-literate fanzine and half-formed punk ethics.

He was pragmatic and decisive, always able to cut through our hyperbole and woolly thinking and give a straight answer to a fuzzy question. Like Coke he was the real thing – what you saw on the stage was essentially a larger-than-life extension of the man.

Lee's fist-thumping delivery had, it turned out, been heavily influenced by having once seen the legendary Chicago bluesman Howlin' Wolf. Some are born to play the king, some to play the fool: Brilleaux chose the demented car salesman from hell who wasn't so much selling his wares but ramming them down your throat.

In later years, the Feelgoods gradually assumed a less prominent role in my life. Pub-rock had become an interesting historical footnote and punk had turned into something really frightening called New Romanticism. The Feelgoods settled down into a familiar routine of grafting and recording,

ticking over like a well-tuned engine and clocking up at least 200 gigs a year.

By the start of the 1990s, Lee Brilleaux was the only original member left. It was about this time that I ran into him again, standing uncomfortably alone in an unfamiliar Soho watering hole. He didn't know anyone, no-one knew him. Of course, he didn't remember me but, sensing a chance to step out of the unfamiliar pub and have a quick chat with anyone, he came outside and we finished our pints in the bright summer glare. He was, it transpired, *en route* to Germany for yet another 30 dates. Doing what comes naturally, taking care of business. As ever he was avuncular and approachable, just as over ten years before.

Sometime in '93, the rumour mill leaked the fact that Lee Brilleaux was poorly. Off the road. Serious. Soon this unpleasant rumour was announced as a fact: Lee Brilleaux had cancer. In early '94 Brilleaux fronted the band again to make a live recording at the Feelgood Music Bar on Canvey. Perhaps, I thought, things weren't as bad as they seemed.

Little over three months later I opened up a newspaper to see an unexpected picture of Lee Brilleaux…on an obituary page. He had died on 7 April 1994, aged 41. The obituary in *The Telegraph*, of all places, rounded off by saying that Lee was 'a credit both to Essex man and the venerable traditions of British R&B.'

When I now listen to what turned out to be the last recordings of Brilleaux fronting his band, I get a renewed sense of the sheer power and guts of the man. The sensationally moody 'Wolfman Callin'', for example, contains one of the best harp solos Lee ever laid down on tape, a screaming, bawling racket replete with stinging high notes.

Elsewhere on the set you can hear him gruffly shouting orders into the mic just like he always did. These recordings were Brilleaux's swansong. A typically tough collection of standards and originals barked out to an appreciative audience as only Brilleaux could. Right to the end he had class, he had style.

It is in that spirit that the current well-tuned line-up are continuing to play and entertain the public all over the world. Carrying on the tradition, taking care of business which was Lee's final wish.

CANVEY

If you go down to Canvey Island today, you'll find the Dr Feelgood office located, appropriately enough, above a betting shop in a rather bland-looking parade of shops. Inside the basic and strictly functional four-roomed office there's a desk, a phone, a map of Europe tacked on the wall and a few filing cabinets which together conspire to make the place look, at first glance, like a typical minicab office. The only evidence of its real purpose comes in the silver albums for 'Malpractice' and 'Stupidity' which hang proudly on the wall.

This office isn't just some convenient short-term rental unit – it is, quite literally, the house that Dr Feelgood built: the firm owns not just the office but the whole block it's set in. This is the centre of operations for the Feelgood camp as it has been for the past 21 years. It is also the address of Grand Records, the band's own label which they formed in 1985 to release new recordings and license back catalogue.

The bloke behind the desk who runs this show is rapidly disappearing behind a pile of faxes with an ever-ringing phone pressed to his ear. Long-time manager Chris Fenwick is man who knows more about the rock'n'roll business than most

people have forgotten. To Chris, the equation is simple. A band is like the four spark plugs in an engine. They must be kept in running order at all times. If one gets 'sooted up' there's no spark…and no spark means no engine.

He's a man who has an inherent understanding of the subtle ways in which rock'n'roll musicians work. For example, he can judge the entire mood of a band stuck out on the road somewhere in the middle of Europe just by checking the time they phone into the office to report on the previous night's gig. An early, pre-midday call usually means good gig, good crowd, band still excited, ready to roll and on the road. Positive. A late-afternoon call equals bad gig, low turnout, band in back of van pissed off. Don't ask.

The Dr Feelgood story is not just a gig-to-gig, record-to-record almanac. It is the story of an R&B firm, an organisation that set up shop 25 years ago and is still open for business. This achievement is in no small measure due to Fenwick and his canny managerial mind, allied with a single-minded determination that's enabled the whole operation to stay afloat through all the inevitable ups and downs. As Will Birch observes about the Feelgood camp, 'In the early days, Chris was inexperienced but he rose to the challenge. In later days he was the mastermind. Lee did it on stage and Chris did it on the phone, it was a brilliant partnership.'

Thanks to this unique tenacity, Dr Feelgood as an operation have survived and thrived long after the prolonged honeymoon of the early days was over – and this in a business where people come and go out of fashion overnight. To still be running the show after 30 years is, in many ways, just plain out of order. But Fenwick isn't expecting a gold watch from anyone.

From the off, Dr Feelgood was always conceived and established as a gigging act which was virtually never off the road. Every year they would be out on tour constantly, knocking out over

200 shows. It was a blueprint for success they stuck with for the next two decades. Yet this relentless touring schedule was to exact a price. Relationships in the band were tested and pushed to their limits, as was the physical resolve of others as they struggled with the dull realities involved in getting on to a different stage night after night for months at a time.

Somehow the Feelgoods have transcended all the slings and arrows and emerged stronger and more vibrant than ever. They still evoke the spirit and the ethos of those unforgettable nights spent down the front at the Kursaal or at one of many Top Ranks on the circuit across the UK They remain, as Nick Lowe put it with typical economy, 'the greatest local band in the world.'

Laaadeeez and gentlemen put your hands together! From Canvey Island, Essex. Doctor Feelgood...

The Feelgoods – still in business in the new millennium. From left, Steve Walwyn, Robert Kane, Kevin Morris, Phil Mitchell.

THE TIN CAN CARAVAN MEN 2

Like all the best *Boy's Own* adventure stories, this one starts on a mysterious island. Dr Feelgood emerged from two very distinct musical traditions that had existed on Canvey for years just waiting to bump into each other. Its roots stretch back to the early 1960s, a whole decade before 19 year old singer Lee Collinson and guitarist mate John B Sparkes joined forces with guitarist John Wilkinson and his schoolyard chum, drummer John Martin to hammer out R&B music for their own amusement. Here's how it happened.

Lee Collinson was born in Durban on 10 May 1952. His father was a lathe operator who had travelled out from England to South Africa as part of a general call which had echoed out across the British Empire for skilled labour to come forward and work on fixed-term contracts. As a result of this geographical accident of birth, Lee had a Zulu nanny and was able to speak Swahili before he could speak English.

By the time he was four or five, the family had returned to England where they lived for a while in the less than exotic London suburb of Ealing before decamping to Canvey in the mid-1960s. Forty minutes by train from Fenchurch Street, Canvey Island always had close contacts with London and particularly with the East End. During the war, blitzed families had been evacuated there and after the hostilities they habitually returned to spend their summer holidays. Lee's grandfather already lived on the island and the family would come down from London to enjoy their vacations with him.

The South Side Jug Band comprised, from left, Harry Ashcroft, Lew Lewis, Chris White, John B Sparkes and (foreground) Lee Collinson on the banjo.

15

It was during this period that Lee first tied up with long-time friend Chris White, to whom he was always 'the boy who came from London'. It was through him that Lee also became introduced to another neighbourhood kid, John Sparkes. When Lee's parents built a house a short distance away from Chris White's parents, Lee was installed at the local Sweyne grammar school and settled down to a new way of life.

The relatively uncrowded and communal Canvey scene in the early 1960s afforded kids a perfect adventure playground across which they could roam with impunity. Being below sea level with nothing but a sea wall to protect it from regular flooding, it had a natural affinity with all things to do with water and boats and both Lee and Chris would constantly be found playing on the creeks and inlets near their homes in their own small rowing boats which they could launch straight into the sea from their back gardens. The small sandbars and banks which surround this reclaimed spot of land, dotted with old chains and bits and pieces of old boats, quickly became an exciting landscape on which children's minds could go to work. Islands, after all, meant only one thing – treasure – and treasure islands meant pirates and secret maps.

It was Lee who spent some considerable time drawing out a full-colour scale map of this secret domain complete with gangs of marauding pirates, seagulls and treasure chests. Where 'X' marked the spot, the two lads established their own private and suitably inaccessible camp way out on a sandbank known as Long Horse Island in Benfleet Creek. This secret base, called 'The Hut' and constructed on piles sunk deep into the sand, could only be reached by boat and entered via a hole in the floor. Here the lads would muck about, have barbecues, light bonfires and generally make plans to lay waste the whole of North Kent in a series of secret waterborne raids. Later on, when they had graduated to boats fitted with outboard motors, their domain extended over the busy Thames estuary into North Kent and the sinister fortress of Hadleigh Castle.

As Chris simply says of those halcyon days, 'We were Marsh Rats.' One day Lee took himself on a boat trip across the fast-flowing Thames Estuary and hit the coast of North Kent for the day. The problems came on the return journey when his small outboard motor was no match against the ebb tide and he started to be swept out to sea. Eventually he had to be rescued by the lifeboat. Bloody kids.

Johnny Kidd and his Pirates, a seminal influence on the young Wilko Johnson.

While this distinctly 'Swallows and Amazons' lifestyle was being pursued on one part of the island, a slightly older young man, 16 year old John Wilkinson, was also playing pirates. Only he was doing it on his turntable in the form of archetypal British beat boomers Johnny Kidd and the Pirates.

Like most guitar-obsessed teenagers at the time, young Wilko had spent the usual hours locked away in his bedroom trying to get his fingers around various Hank Marvin/Shadows riffs. He'd put these to work in his first ever band the Roamers, which he'd formed along with John Martin, a schoolmate who was keen on learning to play the drums.

A picture taken for the *Canvey and Benfleet Recorder* shows an enthusiastic-looking pop band larking about. The year is 1964 and the guitarist with the neat cut hair is recognisably Wilkinson, leaning forward to admire a flat-capped Martin performing an impromptu roll on the snare drum while lying on the ground. The Roamers used to play local youth clubs and even old folks' homes – an arrangement which came through John Martin's parents, themselves somewhat musical,

who encouraged Wilko and John to join them. As Figure recalls today, 'It was bizarre – but any chance to play a drum and a guitar was great.'

It wasn't until he first heard Johnny Kidd and the Pirates, to some the most authentic and original rock'n'roll group Britain ever produced, that Wilko's ears opened to the sound of something very new and exciting. As he was later to recall, the track 'I'll Never Get Over You' was the clincher. 'I heard this song over the radio and the guitar break just transfixed me. I realised that this guitar-playing was like nothing I'd ever heard. I also got the feeling that this was the real thing, real R&B, although it was a complete pop song. It was just so obviously better than anything Merseybeat guitarists were doing.'

Young Wilko had found himself a mentor, an authentic hero he could try and emulate. His name was Mick Green, the Pirates' guitarist who'd evolved a style which made it possible to effectively play rhythm and lead at the same time by strumming without a pick. It was because of Green that Wilko, when he could afford it, settled on the Fender Telecaster as his chosen weapon,

The Roamers line up for the camera, from left, Larry Freeman (vocals), John Martin, Wilko Johnson, Terry Hounsom (bass) and Ian Southey (rhythm guitar).

Above: Wilko and his treasured Telecaster.

Below: The Razzamatazz Washboard Band with caravan and pram. Harry Ashcroft stands at rear with Sparko, Chris and Lee, with Rico Burt (washboard) and Mick Townsend (bass).

the tips of his fingers dancing Green-style across the hair-trigger strings.

Wilko recalls that at the time his mum wouldn't let him take out a hire-purchase loan on such an expensive item, so he persuaded the shop to hold onto it while he paid it off a week at a time. At least, he figured, it was his. Finally his girlfriend Irene succumbed, paid off the last payments and Wilko had his dream come true – a Fender Telecaster in a velvet-lined case. And Irene? He married the gal.

In time the Roamers evolved into an outfit called the North Avenue Jug Band, a skiffle group which used to busk out on the streets featuring Wilko, his brother Malco and a couple of other local lads. John Martin meanwhile threw his lot in with various other Canvey/Southend groups such as the Essex Five, which were still very much influenced by the Beatles and the Shadows.

One day at a carnival talent contest, three very enthusiastic boys came forward to see what was going on. This was, of course, the triumvirate of Lee, Chris and Sparko. 'I was about 18 at the time and they were about 13 or 14, which at that age is a big gap,' Wilko recalls. 'They were very interested in what we were doing and we were telling them about this music. I remember Lee having a very striking personality; although he was much younger than me, he seemed pretty together.'

Suitably impressed, the magnificent three duly trotted off and, arming themselves with all manner of home-made and scavenged instruments, formed themselves along with a few other likely lads into something called the South Side Jug Band. This hit the streets of Canvey busking in 1967.

If you take a look at the back cover of the Feelgoods' 1979 LP 'Let It Roll', the band are pictured behind the bar of their own drinking club located in what was known as Feelgood House. On the shelf behind Lee Brilleaux's head is a small, framed, black-and-white picture of a bunch of lads somewhere out in the woods earnestly holding a pose in front of a dilapidated caravan. They look like white trash lost in the depths of some mangrove swamp in the Louisiana bayou – only this wasn't the US of A, it was somewhere in the woods of North Kent.

'It was Lee's idea to form a jug band,' recalls Sparko. 'He'd invented this eight-string guitar which was tuned like a banjo. We used to stay in one of them caravans over weekends and then go busking in pubs all over Kent.' The outfit used to move their home-made equipment around using pushbike with an adapted pram (also in the picture) welded onto it like a sidecar.

Sparko also remembers how the band operated in those days: 'We used to get a train from Benfleet and get off at Gravesend and cross over to Kent on the ferry and then it was off to the caravan on the bike/pram. What we did then was one would ride the bike for a few miles and the other would walk

and then the other would leave the bike and set off walking until the other caught up.'

The picture speaks volumes. It evokes a kind of mythical Dennis Potter-like childhood, the sort that parents of today feel that their own children have, in many ways, been cheated out of in an ever-changing and increasingly cynical world. The tall gangly kid proudly leaning a banjo on his leg is Lee, while to his right sporting a 12-string and wearing a well spivvy snap-brimmed fedora is Sparko. Behind them, standing in the doorway of the caravan, is a kid proudly cradling a jug in his arm – Chris. There are other similar snaps taken around the same time picturing the various line-ups of these bands, all which seem to suggest a bunch of lads who are having the time of their lives mucking about with home-made drums, washboards, a jug bass and the odd guitar. Unconsciously learning the tricks of the trade and laying down the foundations of something better.

An insight into where their minds may have been when these happy snaps were taken came from Lee looking back in '77 '...though I am passionately in love with American black music I have broadened a lot. Since Dr Feelgood started, I have realised that I am a white geezer from England, not a bloke from America from the ghetto or something.' Looking back at these pictures today, you sense that a love affair with both music and the imagery it evokes had already started.

The South Side Jug Band was, in fact, just one of several names that the boys used to operate under as they moved around from venue to venue across Canvey and North Kent. Sometimes they would be the Razzamatazz Washboard Band, perhaps the Frisco Bay Jug Band or even simply Chrissy White and His Mad Mates. The band had a definite gigging plan which involved five or six different stints over a typical weekend at venues such as the Canvey Club, the Corner Club and the Oyster Fleet – venues packed with hardworking types from the local gas terminals and fishing communities.

Chris recalls the strategy: 'We went busking outside these pubs and eventually they'd say come inside, a Saturday evening for us would start off at the Corner Club, go in and do four songs, then go over the road and do 15 minutes at the Canvey Club and then go off and do an hour at the Oyster. Sunday we'd do youth clubs and the Canvey Club again.' This was an invaluable apprenticeship for all that was to come, giving everyone the confidence to get up and sing and play – and to hand the hat around afterwards. As a result, by the time they were 14 and 15 years old the lads had probably already clocked up over 200 gigs: they didn't know it then, but they were already behaving like professionals.

Someone who really *was* a pro at the time was drummer John Martin. After the Roamers had split he had concentrated on his drumming, often playing with several bands at the same time. As Figure puts it 'I was in various casual bands at the time and...earning a living at it. I'd go up to Manchester or Liverpool for a long weekend and come back with enough money for the week to live on. They were all bands that were really going nowhere, just pop covers bands.'

The Frisco Bay Jug Band. Back row, from left, Geoff Shaw, Mick Townsend, Lee and Sparko. Front row: Rico Burt and Chris.

Wilko, meanwhile, had graduated from the jug band to the Flowerpots, a group from the Southend area who took their lead from the Orioles, one of the great Southend groups of the time which featuring near-legendary songwriter Mickey Jupp. With Wilko on board, they played Bo Diddley songs and other R&B material. The band's ever-fluctuating line-up included at various times a pianist by the name of John Potter and a keen-as-mustard drummer called Will Birch. By the time they had departed, the Flowerpots had become a guitar-based trio knocking out note-for-note Pirates tunes to their hearts desire.

All this gigging and blues talk was beginning to have a definite effect on the developing character and persona of Master Lee Collinson. He had already subscribed to *Blues Unlimited* magazine and was starting to collect as many American blues records as he could lay his hands on. One day, he heard the news that the American Chicago blues legend Howlin' Wolf was actually coming over to play a gig – in Romford of all places. His mind made up, Lee immediately called Chris White, by now attending a school in London, and told him about the gig. There was simply no way they were going to miss *this* one.

It was to prove to be a decisive moment in the boys' lives. Chris recalls the scenario 'It was a summer's evening, a shitty club with an element of duffel coat in the crowd…' Chris had turned up straight from school decked out in his uniform. 'So there was sunlight streaming through the windows, a shitty hall, a shitty stage in a backroom of a pub with absolutely no atmosphere and then this great monster geezer came out, this huge great black man in a suit, braces and a shirt – absolutely no glitz whatsoever – and just went to work.'

From nothing, the atmosphere in the room suddenly electrified as the Wolfman pounded through a set of definitive Chicago blues tracks – 'Little Red Rooster', 'Ain't Superstitious' and 'Wang Dang Doodle'. Finally, as Chris recalls it, 'he put the harmonica he was playing and the microphone into his mouth and gyrated across the stage.' To coin a phrase a 'mind blown is a mind shown' and Lee Collinson, like Wilko before him, had found something special that he could adapt for his own purposes.

It was around this time that Lee first tried out the harmonica for himself, setting about the task with his usual style. 'I never went out and bought it with the idea that I should learn to play it, the first day I bought it I was playing it. I never consciously sat down and played any instrument to become a virtuoso on it, my slide or my singing. I just used to play for my own pleasure…'

Back in the schoolyard, Lee was already gaining a bit of a reputation for being something of a flamboyant character himself. Current Feelgoods drummer Kevin Morris, who was in the year below, recalls that even then Lee used to sport a waistcoat and a fob watch on a chain and used to move about the school surrounded by a small group of acolytes. 'He wasn't a prefect or anything, probably because he was a bit naughty, but he'd come up to you and ask to see your homework diary and take it off you and tear it up.'

Kevin was later admitted into the inner sanctum when he joined the 'gang' behind the swimming pool and started blasting away on fags. As Kevin puts it, 'Even then he had this big charisma. He commanded this gang, (though) not in a physical sense: it was like he was the spokesperson and he always had a line or a funny quip to deliver to the teachers or anyone else. Because Lee was an only child and his family moved around a lot, his grandmother had a really important role in bringing Lee up. Consequently for a young man he was always taught more adult-type things right

from the off, like how to boil potatoes or how to cook a joint of beef. By the time he was 14 or 15 he was very confident and sussed. To the other bands in the area he had a benevolent, almost godfather-like approach.'

Another former pupil who can recall this aspect of Lee's character is current Dr Feelgood bass player Phil Mitchell, who remembers clearly his own first ever schooldays gig with a band he and a few others had put together. In a burst of naive enthusiasm they'd rehearsed a short set of songs, booked a hall and sold a load of tickets. Come the evening of the gig the hall was packed full with expectant friends and locals. Phil and the boys hit the stage and, fuelled by nervous energy alone, polished off their intended set in something like a quarter of the usual time. As the curtains closed there were still ominously at least two hours left to fill.

While Phil and mates nervously pondered the empty stage, a character suddenly appeared backstage who was clearly savouring the predicament. 'Run out of songs have we, lads?' said Lee, a big grin on his face. With a full hall left expectantly waiting for something else to happen, Phil and band desperately asked Lee the $64,000-question 'What do we do next?' With that, Lee disappeared off into the audience and started to pull in a few faces he knew. In a short time a scratch band was assembling behind the curtains and getting ready to take the stage.

Finally strapping on a guitar, Lee smashed the neck off a beer bottle, shoved it on his finger and took the stage, tearing into all manner of blues classics from 'Dust My Broom' onwards. He had effectively saved the day, turning the evening into a sudden and resounding success. 'Without Lee,' Phil asserts, 'we would have been lynched.' After the gig Phil offered him the 25 quid pot from the door which, with typical style, he declined.

Meanwhile 1967's Summer of Love was kicking in across the country and Wilko was becoming restless. He had been getting by on a few gigs here and there, backed up with all manner of casual dead-end jobs. After the Flowerpots split, he found himself for a fleeting moment in a band called the Fix playing Tamla and soul material. It wasn't for Wilko, who by now had already made his mind up about his immediate future. That autumn, he put his treasured Telecaster guitar back into its case, shoved it under the bed and headed off to Newcastle University to read English. As Hugo Williams put it, Wilko had somewhat perversely 'dropped out in reverse'.

The South Side Jug Band was also undergoing line-up changes. Main 'jug man' Chris White had set his mind on becoming the next Olivier and was already off the island attending a drama school in

London. Schooldays were beginning to run out and the South Side Jug Band eventually split, leaving Lee and Sparko to find refuge in the remains of Wilko's old band the Fix. This new line-up was completed by sometime South Side Jug Band harp player Lew Lewis, who himself used to busk solo outside the bingo halls and pubs on Canvey, and guitarist Dave Higgs.

As Lee spelt it out in an interview with the fanzine *Sideburns* in 1977, 'Dr Feelgood comes from two sources: there was me and Sparko, we were playing around Canvey very much into things like busking and that sort of thing, that's how we met people like Lew Lewis cos we were playing outside of boozers, that sort of thing. Then we met up with Dave Higgs and we formed our first sort of electric band. That would have been about the time of the great British blues boom; we were playing blues stuff along with some Cream numbers all that sort of stuff.' Though the Fix were to prove a short-lived outfit, Dave and Lew would later crop up in teenage punk sensations Eddie and the Hot Rods.

Over on the mainland, pro drummer John Martin was becoming increasingly restless with the bands he was involved in and was slowly gravitating back home. The regular weekend gigs up north still paid the rent but John was getting tired of both the routine and the uninspired material. But at the time there was nothing better on offer. So he stuck to the motorway and kept his ear to the ground.

The next group Lee and Sparko found themselves in was the Pigboy Charlie Band which also went out sometimes as the more explicit Wild Bunch. A sometime drummer in the ever fluctuating line-up was former behind-the-shed smoker Kevin Morris. 'In those days if you had a bass amp or a drum kit you were recruited,' recalls Kev, 'and Lee got me to do a gig with them at the rollerskating rink in Southend.' The fully electric outfit featuring Sparko on guitar and Lee on slide played a set comprised of Elvis, Jerry Lee Lewis and other rock'n'roll classics, travelling from gig to gig in a converted ambulance with the band's name illuminated above the cab. Sparko remembers that as soon as they hit a new town they would cruise up and down the high street on the lookout for girls to impress. Once spotted, the instruction went out to 'flash the Pig light'. It was like a strange mating ritual. The band gigged sporadically in and around Canvey with the occasional foray up the motorway...sometimes to really foreign places like Hitchin!

Once schooldays were finally over, Sparko had taken to the building profession, learning to lay bricks with the best of them, while Lee was encouraged by his mother to start work at a local

firm of solicitors on Canvey as an articled clerk. He hadn't given up playing music, though, and was still collecting all manner of blues records like they were going out of fashion – there was simply no other music he wanted to hear. 'Black music is corrupt, it's corrupting and it's corruptible; that's what makes it so interesting. When I had my straight job working in an office that was my little outlet, I was into R&B and black music of all sorts much more than English rock'n'roll.'

His 'straight job' at the solicitors often involved mundane paperwork, though he'd occasionally be sent to serve a writ on some errant character. On these occasions Lee's boss would instruct him to make sure he never went alone. On one such mission Lee found himself in the unfamiliar surrounds of Piccadilly Circus, heading for Chinatown with a writ destined for some Chinese heavyweight who'd been involved in a heroin-smuggling scam, burning a hole in his pocket. Heeding his boss's advice he gave his mate Chris White a call: if ever he needed back-up, he needed it now.

So it was that the two of them headed into the depths of Soho's Chinatown that afternoon fully expecting to be chased down Gerrard Street by a

When Chris White set his sights on an acting career, he became Chris Fenwick. This is an early publicity shot.

cleaver-wielding Chinaman. In the event they located their man, served the writ and ended up having a friendly cup of China tea in a restaurant with the perpetrator in question. As Chris says of these occasional exploits, 'It was all just another bit of live drama' which they both thrived on.

Indeed Chris' own career as a young actor was beginning to take off. He was being sent along from his drama school to various casting sessions and getting the jobs. Soon he was appearing in such classic TV programmes as *Dixon Of Dock Green*, *Please Sir* and *Z Cars*. In addition to a new career, the young actor had adopted a new identity after the actors' union Equity discovered a Chris White already on their books. They handed him a telephone directory and said 'pick a name.' Chris just elected to use his mother's maiden name, although people who knew him on Canvey still called him Whitey. Another character had been born...

Back on Canvey, as a new decade checked in, an old face was seen around on the island again. Wilko had returned – not only from university, where he had got his degree in English, but also more romantically from a sojourn he'd spent afterwards way out on the 'hippy trail' which stretched across Europe all the way to India. 'A couple of my friends at university had been out there,' Wilko recalls, 'so I thought I would go. Also my father had been out there in colonial times as a regular soldier and I remember him talking about India. I'd never been out of England before, I was really scared. But I had to do it.'

Forced home after contracting a dose of hepatitis, he soon drifted into supply teaching, using his degree to help him earn some money teaching secondary modern kids their O Levels. His guitar, which had remained untouched for years, remained under his bed gathering dust. Lee's career as a clerk was moving on apace: indeed, his boss had arranged for him to attend law school in London once a week to study for his Solicitor's Admission Certificate, the first step in the long road to becoming a brief.

On the musical front, the Pigboy Charlie Band were still doing a few gigs here and there, but as ever suffered from an unstable line-up. It was during one such period that Lee ran into Wilko and then brought him up to speed on what had been going on on the island in the years he had been away.

'He started telling me about this band and how the guitarist had just left,' Wilko remembers, 'and I'm sitting there thinking "mmmm" cos at the time I hadn't played for about three or four years. I had just forgotten about it, really, and I thought I'd like to play, but he didn't have the bottle to ask me and I didn't have the bottle to ask him so we had this

ridiculous conversation where we were both trying to say the same thing.'

Despite this uncharacteristic reticence, wheels had clearly started to turn inside Lee's head. A short while later his lieutenant Sparko turned up on Wilko's doorstep and just said 'Do you want to join our band?' Wilko, by now unable to hide his enthusiasm, said 'Yeah, yeah'.

The new band immediately plugged into the small circuit Pigboy Charlie had been playing – which according to Sparko, was 'British Legion-type clubs and wedding functions' where a bit of Chuck Berry went down very well with a pint and a sausage roll. It was also Sparko who suggested the new band take their name from the old Pirates song 'Dr Feelgood', originally a hit for William 'Piano Red' Perryman ands a popular part of their repertoire. 'Besides,' the bass-man muses, 'the Railway Tavern in Pitsea had been a good gig for us in the past. The landlord had always said to us "If you get a band together give me a call but you must have a name that I can write up on a poster."' Accordingly, they phoned the pub and soon had a regular Sunday residency.

The drumstool at the time was sometimes occupied by Terry Howarth, a local with army band experience whom Lee quickly dubbed 'Bandsman': when he wasn't available, Wilko would ask Flowerpot mate Will Birch to deputise. The band was still very much in its infancy, and there was little to distinguish them from many other similar outfits. 'At that point,' Will Birch recalls, 'Wilko still had very long hair, most of us then were still wearing flares and there was the odd moustache. Most people in bands wanted to be like Eric Clapton or the Rolling Stones.'

However, signs were beginning to show of discontentment with the *status quo*. As Will again puts it, 'there was a slightly underdog stance: they weren't aspiring to be like Uriah Heep, it was a definite "kids on the street" kind of thing. They didn't fit. In 1971-72 nobody was playing R&B. It was totally out of fashion and, with Lee's obsession with blues and Wilko's fixation with the Pirates, it was slowly shaping their music. There were elements of what was to come...'

Will can also recall some early stage antics coming together as they worked out with 'Blue Suede Shoes' at a near-deserted pub. 'Lee was performing like a madman...he'd taken off his own shoes and held them together with the mic stuck into them as if they were singing.'

In addition, as Canvey lads they were already marked out as being different. John Eichler, who later managed the Hope and Anchor in Islington and who himself comes from Southend, says: 'If you were in Southend you were always very paranoid about Canvey boys in general. They could be nasty, they had something of an edge.' Dave Bronze, who later played with and produced the band, agrees: 'That's how people think of Canvey. They are like an Independent State – state being the operative word…'

Back on the mainland, another regular gig for the band was to be the Alexandra Hotel in Southend, popularly known as the Top Alex to distinguish it from another hotel of the same name at the bottom of the high street. The Top Alex had a function room upstairs and Dr Feelgood used to play there on Sundays. Another regular gig in Southend at the time was the Esplanade.

The band were slowly beginning to change and acquire a kind of street image that differed markedly from the run-of-the-mill flares and cheesecloth shirts. A strong influence on them all was one of Lee and Sparko's favourite TV programmes, the American cop show *Hawaii Five-O* which starred the chiselled and ever-tanned features of Jack Lord as detective Steve McGarrett. This programme was the fount from which a dozen great catchphrases sprang from every week. Lee and Sparko couldn't get enough of them and soon phrases like 'Book him Danno' and 'Murder one, two counts' became part and parcel of the in-group banter and general humour that was being tossed about.

Even the sharp-suited image of the Hawaiian police force was something which was being taken on board. Will Birch recalls his younger brother Howard swapping a light-coloured jacket with narrow lapels with Lee, who handed over a well-worn Levi's jacket in return. It was another turning point. 'As soon as Lee put that jacket on he became like someone else.'

The gigs around this time were still fairly local and still down to the band to organise. When they weren't gigging they would sometimes rehearse in an old church hall and use their own ripped-fronted speaker columns for a PA. They also spent a lot of time hanging out at Wilko's house, where he would regale them with stories of his journey to (and his trips in) India. After all, no-one had ever gone that far from Canvey Island before. Hand in hand with this came the inevitable rolling of jazz woodbines.

The soundtrack for these impromptu sessions was supplied by three key LPs which were rarely off the turntable in the Johnson household during that year of 1971: 'J Geils' First', Van Morrison's 'St Dominic's Preview' and Mickey Jupp's 'Red Boot'. Apart from actually gigging, the band had no game plan to speak of – they were simply playing the music they liked for the sheer pleasure and fun of it as they'd always done. Wilko, as yet, wasn't writing material and, as Lee was to put it, 'when Wilko joined, Sparko was a shocking bass player

and I was a terrible singer.' Things could only get better.

Lee's mate Chris Fenwick, meanwhile, had been invited to a wedding of a fellow drama student which was taking place in Holland. Leaping at the chance to go abroad, Chris packed his bag and a box of confetti. At the reception Chris was introduced to the master of ceremonies, an enterprising character called Franz Moerland who'd set up a small music agency to supply DJs and bands across Holland. Seizing the moment, Chris cast himself as a well-known English DJ who, as it happened, knew a very tasty band who were raring to go – and returned to England with the promise of a few paid gigs for both himself and a band.

He put the proposition to Dr Feelgood and, to further ensure the success of the venture, bought a secondhand van to take the band over on the ferry. The only fly in the ointment was the lack of a full-time drummer – and it was at this point that Wilko suggested his old mate John Martin. John already knew the boys anyway, as he was also a regular visitor round at Wilko's place.

The man who'd already attracted the moniker 'The Big Figure' from both Wilko and his brother (on account of his physical stature and, perhaps,

his striking profile) recalls that, at the time, he had been married for about 18 months and was living in a caravan in Chelmsford. 'One day I had this knock on the door and it was Wilko and Chris. They said we've got this band called Dr Feelgood and these gigs in Holland and our drummer is going back into the army – we'd like you to come with us.'

One of the band's first publicity shots with the Canvey landscape, as ever, providing the backdrop.

23

Figure had never been abroad before and so agreed to come along for the ride, do the gigs and see how they went. At the time there was no firm invite to join the band, since he was already working as a professional drummer with Finnean's Rainbow (uncharitably dubbed Flanagan's Flame-throwers by the irrepressible Lee) and the boys felt he was in a different league.

On the Whitsun holiday, when everyone could get a few days off work, Dr Feelgood set sail. Once landed, they immediately attracted the attention of the Dutch police as their van was little more than a death trap on wheels. It was only after Chris had convinced them that the heap would soon be leaving the country again that they were allowed to proceed.

The five or six dates were, as Chris puts it, 'a significant gallop' for a band used to a more sedate one gig a week – and how well they responded. 'There was a chemistry which everyone in the band noticed.' In addition, the promoter was taking care of business and looking after his artistes. Chris: 'You got there and they said right boys here's your 20 beer tickets each, there's a lump of dope, here's some space cakes, there's sandwiches in the dressing rooms and you thought yeah this will do. Plus there were a lot of Dutch girls hanging around and so the whole thing was fun with a capital F. Plus we were getting paid for it.'

The effect was instantaneous. No sooner had they boarded the ferry than Wilko was the first to suggest they should start taking it all more seriously, 'Really give it a go.' Yet at the time it was Lee, who had his job and his day-release law course to think about, who was most unsure. Wilko recalls something of an argument developing. 'I said fucking hell, man, you're 19 years old – let's do it!'

The logic of Wilko's argument was simply that

Lee had nothing to lose. If he gave the band a go and it all failed then he could go back to the job anytime he wanted. This was, as Lee agreed, undeniably true and so from that moment onwards Lee had no argument and Dr Feelgood had become a semi-pro outfit.

The short hop to Holland was quickly followed by another which further convinced everyone that it was really something worth giving a try. Chris Fenwick had become their *de facto* manager and John Martin had quit Finnean's Rainbow, taking a job at Ford's so he could play with the band whenever they had a gig without having to disappear up the M1 every weekend.

But he still wasn't thinking of it in terms of being a professional position. 'I didn't ever think that it had a hope in hell of being successful, I thought it was like a step down the ladder, it was just to take things more easy and play the music I wanted to play.' As Figure puts it now: 'It was Wilko who turned me onto R&B, but it was Lee who turned me onto the blues.'

The singer understood perfectly how the two different factions meshed together so well. 'On the one hand you've got Sparko and me who at that time were very much into the blues and R&B, whereas Wilko and Figure had been brought up much more in the school of rock'n'roll. When the two of us got together there were little compromises which we made without realising that we were making them – plus the fact that Wilko was very much into having a four-piece group of bass, drums, guitar and vocals, which meant that we were limited in what you could do stylistically. In that sense the style was set and the model we had for that was the Pirates, Johnny Kidd and the Pirates, which was an English band playing in the tradition of the blues. It was like all of us coming together.'

3

The stripped-down sound of the Pirates was at least an ideal towards which they could strive, and listening to tough, white, city-boy records like the J Geils Band round at Wilko's house was giving the boys additional encouragement. But one more leg of their apprenticeship had still to be served before they were truly ready to rumble. This was to come in the form of an unlikely alliance that was forged between the young, enthusiastic Feelgoods and an almost forgotten star from the glory days of the early 1960s. The name of this icon was Heinz.

Heinz Burt was best known for his glittering past as a former member of the 1960s outfit the Tornados in which he'd played bass guitar. For a time the group also operated as Billy Fury's backing band before having a massive chart success with the groundbreaking instrumental 'Telstar', produced and written by legendary pop Svengali Joe Meek.

After the Tornados, Heinz set about trying to establish himself as a solo act. With his distinctive blonde-haired quiff he certainly looked like an authentic rock'n'roller and managed to translate it all into a couple of hit records, 'Just Like Eddie' and

'Country Boy', both of which came out in 1963. After this Heinz's star waned somewhat and he gradually retreated to the safety of the revival circuit where he cropped up at one-off gigs all over the country.

Though Heinz's main source of income in the early 1970s came from selling classified advertising at the *Southend Evening Echo*, he often needed a pick-up band to go out on the road with him. By the time the Feelgoods had come back from Holland the second time they were very much 'going for it' – the only problem was 'it' wasn't going for them. Gigs were still sporadic and local, and nothing much had changed. So when Heinz contacted them and suggested that they back him for a few dates it seemed like a good idea.

The younger Feelgoods saw Heinz as an experienced hand who at least had a few paying gigs to offer. As Wilko now puts it, 'This way we could at least get gigs at Teddy-boy clubs and places like that – and if we went out backing him we could earn a bit more money than we could on our own.' With added piano from former Flowerpot man John Potter to fill out the sound, Heinz had found himself a backing band.

The Feelgoods' line-up that backed Heinz, seen posing with Chris Fenwick's father's Mercedes, included pianist John Potter (second from left).

Nowadays Heinz would be the sort of person that might be described as being 'a bit of a character'. Wilko, putting it a bit more pointedly although still with a wry chuckle in his voice, calls him 'a talent-free zone.' The first rehearsal that the band turned up to quickly dispelled any preconceptions that the lads were harbouring about their new frontman.

Figure recalls that the Feelgoods would trot keenly round to his house for what they imagined would be a 'full-blown rehearsal, like go through all the songs – but basically all he did was say "yeah, that one is in A". Wilko would hit a chord and then he'd go "yeah, that's fine" and move onto the next one. We were completely stunned because we were looking up to Heinz as being a star and the bubble burst a little bit…but he was great fun.'

The brief association with Heinz provided innumerable 'on the road' anecdotes which the members of the band still laugh at today. Heinz used to meet the band on the day of a gig at a pub called the Army and Navy in Chelmsford, hiding behind the wall in the car park and waiting for a pre-arranged hoot from the Feelgood van before he would reveal himself. The reason for this cloak-and-dagger approach was, Figure recalls, entirely due to the fact that the blonde bombshell was 'totally paranoid about losing his job, He just didn't want to be spotted by anyone taking time off work.'

The actual gigs were organised so that the Feelgoods would open up with their own 40-minute set, as Wilko remembers it 'sticking pretty close to Chuck Berry and Eddie Cochran material rather than R&B.' At a certain point, Lee would announce 'Ladies and Gentlemen…Heinz'. Heinz would then take the stage and take the microphone while Lee, often joined by Chris Fenwick, would do the backing vocals.

However, things didn't always go according to plan, since while the Feelgoods were warming up his audience Heinz was known to prepare himself backstage for performance by putting away several bottles of highly potent barley wine, his favourite tipple. One night at a gig in Sheffield where the band supported Mungo Jerry, Lee did the usual honours and announced Heinz, who promptly crashed through the back curtain and knocked over one of Figure's cymbal stands. The edge of the cymbal cut straight through a power line, plunging the entire stage into darkness!

Once in the van and out on the road Heinz would, with boring regularity, always ask his protégés the same routine question about the night's gig. He would hold up two sparkly stage costumes – one white, one black – and ask everyone which one he should wear that night. Whatever one the band suggested usually resulted

in Heinz picking the other! One particular night, as Sparko recalls, Heinz had a surprise up his sleeve. 'He said I've got a great idea, I'm going to wear both costumes with the white one concealed underneath the black and when we get to the middle eight of "Whole Lotta Shakin' Goin' On" I'm going to whip the black suit off and return in a moment in a different costume…the audience will be amazed.'

On the night, the band duly strode into the instrumental break and Heinz left the stage for his miraculous quick change. Unfortunately, and perhaps due to the barley wine, he failed to return for almost ten minutes as he manfully struggled to extract his legs from the clinging trousers. By the time he'd triumphantly returned to the stage in a different costume nobody in the audience was any the wiser!

Despite such rigours of the road, the Feelgoods were at least playing regularly and extending their gigging range beyond the familiar Canvey/Southend scene. Will Birch swears that Heinz, a keen angler, used to organise his dates around the country according to their proximity to various well-stocked rivers. He'd sometimes go off at night after a gig looking for something exotic lurking in the nearby deep, the resulting catch travelling around in the back of the van with everyone else for a few days until he got back home.

For the Feelgoods the pinnacle of the Heinz days was undoubtedly the 1972 Wembley Rock'n'Roll Festival, whose bill included names like Chuck Berry, Jerry Lee Lewis and Bo Diddley. And even though Heinz was due to go on in the broad daylight of the early afternoon while the cavernous football stadium was still slowly filling up, it was by far the biggest venue the Feelgoods had ever played. Just to be on the same bill as some of the names involved was in itself a thrill. As Chris recalls the prevailing mood of everyone: 'This is what dreams are made of. I'm 18 years old and I'm backstage with Chuck Berry.' Wilko even managed to get the great man to autograph his Telecaster.

The band were naturally quite nervous, and Wilko recalls the event as if it were yesterday. 'It was just mad, it was chaotic, the monitors weren't working – although I didn't really know what monitors were – and I'm standing on stage thinkin' this isn't happening…it's *mental*.' As part of his stage presentation that day Heinz had decided to add a few Elvis-like karate kicks in the solo breaks. One of these inadvertently hit the end of Wilko's guitar, knocking it totally out of tune, while the rest of the band soldiered on. Without the guitar to hold it all together they lost it completely, leaving Wilko standing on stage at Wembley manfully

Two big names of the past – Heinz (left), whom the embryonic Feelgoods backed, and the MC5 (below) with whom they shared the bill at 1972's Wembley Rock'n'Roll Festival. Note the similarity of the monochrome album sleeve to 'Down By The Jetty'.

trying to re-tune his guitar from scratch. It was a baptism of fire which the band never forgot.

Despite this cock-up, the day was to prove memorable for the appearance of Detroit's proto-punks the MC5 featuring the twin-guitar attack of Fred 'Sonic' Smith and Wayne Kramer. Compared to what else was on offer that day these boys were very different. As Figure recalls 'they were very impressive to look at. They were fierce and mean – for a start the guitarist had his face painted gold, he wore a black suit and shades.' This garb was not exactly what the ultra-conservative Teds would call either rock or roll or even acceptable, and bottles and tins were soon raining down on the stage as the band zipped through such gems as 'Tutti Frutti', 'Teenage Lust' and even 'The Human Being Lawnmower'.

Wilko connected with the MC5 immediately. 'I was wandering back and forwards under the stage and I saw this band. You could see straight away that they were very self-confident.' Apart from the striking appearance of the guitarists, Wilko also noted the way in which one of them jerked around

the stage in a series of sudden movements. 'I thought, yeah, I like that. It taught me a thing or two…'

This gig was to be the effective final parting of the ways between Heinz and the Feelgoods. Pianist John Potter decamped and the four-piece line-up was settled. All in all, the Heinz experience had proved something of an education. Listening to the litany of rip-offs and wheeler-dealings that had happened to Heinz over the years convinced the band of one very simple fact which was to stick in all their minds – and particularly in the developing business mind of Chris Fenwick. 'It wasn't going to happen to us.'

Back on the circuit and still searching for some sense of stage presence, Wilko suggested that they take a page from the MC5's book and try a dab of greasepaint. Using some of Chris's knowledge of theatrical make-up, the band did a few gigs which featured Wilko with a gold-painted face and Lee and Sparko in matching silver, Figure refusing point-blank to participate in an experiment that was quickly forgotten. Nevertheless, the band were still experimenting, trying to develop an onstage image for themselves that was not only comfortable to live with but also different enough to get them noticed.

As Lee was to put it some years later, 'When we started playing we didn't move about at all…when people ask me about the stage act I can't remember because it just came gradually. Bit by bit people would try things and every night it would exaggerate itself and take itself a step further. The thing is to excite yourself as much as the audience.' In that respect, they were about to excel themselves.

ROLLING AND TUMBLING

4

After splitting with Heinz, the band continued on the local circuit they'd been working for the past year or so, venues like the Palace Bar Rooms in Southend and the Cloud Nine Disco on Canvey Sea Wall being interspersed with the odd airbase and college outing. Meanwhile, less than an hour up the A13, something of a musical revolution was beginning to get under way in the capital's hostelries.

Pub-rock, as the media labelled it, began as a reaction to the progressive rock boom that had erupted in the late 1960s and went on to dominate the early 1970s music scene. Inspired by the example of Eggs Over Easy and Brinsley Schwarz at the Tally Ho pub in London's Kentish Town, bands playing a softer, more melodic and song-based music were starting to attract record company interest.

A small booking agency called the Iron Horse was formed to push many of these new acts forward, the intention being to open up a gig circuit using pubs dotted across London, most of which had a small backroom or a stage stuck in a corner going to waste. Once established, landlords quickly became convinced of the sound economic sense of the venture, and by 1973 a small but thriving circuit of pub venues had been established that included the Tally Ho in Kentish Town, the Kensington in West Kensington and the Hope and Anchor, Islington. Most of the gigs were free to get into and if there was a full bar it was a very convivial atmosphere to both see and hear a band.

Soon these small gigs were slowly beginning to attract press interest. Reviews were starting to crop up in the pages of *Melody Maker* and *New Musical Express* and the band noticed by a much wider audience of punters and music-business types alike. Someone who was well aware of this burgeoning scene was former Feelgood deputy drummer Will Birch, who was by this time pursuing his own musical plans. He had just formed a group that, in October, would become the Kursaal Flyers (of 'Little Does She Know' fame). He got the Feelgoods their first London gig, and in August 1974 they'd return the favour.

Have American car, will travel – the Feelgoods' 1973 promotional shot.

Birch's contact was Dai Davies a charismatic Welshman who'd cut his teeth working for David Bowie and the MainMan organisation. Apart from managing Ducks Deluxe, he was involved in a music agency which booked bands into several pub venues and Birch started to pester him about his mates back on Canvey. Dai, with half an ear on ten other phonecalls, promised he'd give them a go.

Will: 'It was always about to happen, this would have been around February/March '73, and it always got cancelled at the last minute. I think Dai wanted to put them on but he was looking for a suitable slot. Wilko used to say to me "this gig doesn't seem to have materialised, then…"'

After several false starts, a date was suddenly firmed up when Ducks Deluxe, booked into play at the Tally Ho, had the offer of a more prestigious gig. Dai needed a band fast to fill the date and the Feelgoods had their London debut at last. So it was that in the summer of '73 Dr Feelgood loaded up their transit and headed up the A13 bound for the capital.

Even though the venue was only a boozer, it was a boozer in London – a place quite beyond the Feelgoods' collective experience. Will Birch: 'We all went up to London to see this momentous occasion. There were about 40 or 50 in the audience and the set was all R&B. The Feelgoods weren't daunted by London but I think Lee had reservations. I don't think he expected it to lead to anything and it was all played down a bit in case it went wrong.'

The band were still rough and ready, Wilko still had a head of long hair and there were as yet no original songs in the set. Even so, the Feelgoods impressed Dai Davies sufficiently to secure a booking at the Lord Nelson in the Holloway Road within a fortnight. Dr Feelgood had, it seemed, arrived in the big city…and pretty soon it would have trouble containing them.

It was in this initial period that the band really tightened up as a musical unit – and, almost as importantly, as a theatrical act, developing the moves that were to play such a vital role in their early recognition. Wilko: 'We never ever once discussed the act or tried to work it out. It was something which evolved…Lee had his vibe and I could work off it.'

A publicity shot at the time shows the 1973 look of the band. Taken on a road somewhere on Canvey, the boys hold a typical pose round a borrowed American car. Though Lee, Sparko and Figure all have full heads of hair, Wilko is out on his own and strikingly different with distinctly unfashionable-looking suit and a much shorter barnet. Once again, it seemed, someone was dropping out in reverse.

Another part of the inherent appeal of the band was their nicotine and sawdust mystique. After all, to most average Londoners Canvey Island was as obscure a place as you could name. The Feelgoods had arrived on the London scene overnight without a track record and were, in many ways, the last of a dying breed – a group of mates from out of town who had just formed a band. Nobody knew them, and they stood out like typical Canvey lads as a breed apart.

They didn't dress in the same in regulation jeans and denim waistcoats: they looked harder, shiftier – an image that, combined with their nicknames, made them seem more exotic than they really were. Wilko, after all, was better than John, as was Sparko and Big Figure. Lee had, by this time, acquired the nickname Brillo, possibly after the iron wool pan-scourer. Chris Fenwick suggests that this was probably down to the state of his hair after one particularly hectic gig when someone had quipped that 'it looks like a Brillo pad'. True or not Lee decided to 'Frog it up' by adding a more resonant 'eaux' to the end which fitted right in with his enjoyment of all things Cajun and Zydeco.

It was after they'd established a foothold on the London circuit with regular weekly gigs that things started to move very quickly indeed. The pub circuit was very much a word-of-mouth environment where anything slightly new or different soon had the bush telegraph buzzing. The Feelgoods were marked out right from the start, firstly because not only were they playing rather unfashionable R&B music as opposed to the much more crafted American style of country-rock favoured by their contemporaries, but also because they just looked and acted more aggressively. Characterising a typical pub-rock band of the time, Dai Davies recalls that 'they tended to stand around in a circle on stage being muso-ish, whereas the Feelgoods looked like bit part players from *The Sweeney*.'

If London had one single overriding effect on the band, it was to make them more professional. Figure recalls that 'Lee developed a much meaner attitude on stage, Sparko was just, well, Sparko, and one night Wilko started to skit about on stage in overdrive – and the reaction to that was quite incredible.'

For Will Birch, it was the overall look and attitude of the band which really did the job for them right from the off. 'If they had looked like the Pretty Things or the Grease Band it wouldn't have happened because the music by itself wasn't distinctive enough.' It's Will's further assertion that if you take any successful rock'n'roll act then 80 per cent of their impact is based on how they look.

He cites a list as long as your arm from Elvis, through to the Sex Pistols and the Clash to back his claim that 'Rock'n'roll is a visual medium first and foremost, and the Feelgoods were more visual than anyone else in the country at the time...the stage was their habitat and their impact was a shock. It was the shock of the new...they presented some familiar music in a way that was totally new.'

As each new piece of stage business was tried and tested in front of a growing, slack-jawed and very enthusiastic audience, the act developed apace. Lee's trousers narrowed, Wilko's suits got blacker, Fig's hair became greased back and Sparko clung onto his cheap-looking, fully-flared wedding suits for all he was worth. The music, image and the intention was sparse and pared-down in a way no-one in the audience had ever come across before. Not since the early 1960s when the Who and the Rolling Stones had gigged round London had anyone experienced such an 'in your face' presentation.

With each foray up to London the band grew both in stature and in confidence. Will Birch: 'They weren't tainted and disillusioned by it all. They could get into London, strike and get out – and it was during that van drive to and from London that you develop a real "us and them" attitude, like you're a little gang going up to London to do your stuff.' Recalling the vibe of the time, Wilko adds 'When things started happening I'd start to think that what we were doing was a bit of a crusade, thinking about some of the crap that was going on at the time like Emerson Lake and Palmer...it felt a bit like we were trying to destroy all that.'

It was evidently a feeling shared by half the pub-goers of London not to mention the writers at *Melody Maker* and *New Musical Express* who were, by the early 1970s, getting desperate for

something new to start happening. Suddenly it was.

The key to understanding the appeal and impact the group had at the time comes in an interview which Lee gave to Neil Spencer of the *NME* in mid-1975. When asked about the nature of the Feelgood stage act, Lee replied 'That's one reason why I like working with an outfit this size, it means you have to give your all every time...'

Q: Every time?

A: 'Yeah, it's a golden rule with the Feelgoods that you give your last bit to every gig. It has to be.'

In other press around the time which similarly sought to probe the deeper meanings behind the Feelgoods' very upfront 'no philosophy philosophy', Figure confided to one journo that he liked playing the drums because he 'enjoyed hitting things', while Lee let slip that he enjoyed singing the way he did because he 'liked shouting'.

With this plain wrapper, no-holds-barred attitude at work, the name Dr Feelgood was soon on every hip lip in London. Dai Davies describes them now as having been '...visually riveting, really dangerous.' John Eichler, who at the time managed the band Help Yourself, says 'that when they played they ripped everyone apart...it was like a bush fire...' and best of all Charles Shaar Murray, of the *NME*, succinctly likened their act to 'Hiroshima in a pint mug.'

In the London pub circuit the Feelgoods found

a vibrant and expectant audience who they could take with them. The combined past musical experiences of each member now came into play as they honed the act until it was razor-sharp and quite simply unmissable. The band would turn up at a place like the Kensington which, as Chris Fenwick recalls, was 'the most uninspiring boozer ever – to say it was dull would be an understatement. It was a real zero, the stage was useless.' Once the Feelgoods were on it, everything changed.

The quickly developing Brilleaux stage persona was an adaptation from Howlin' Wolf out of Romford – full-frontal, fist-punching, pulsating. When he wasn't actually shouting into the microphone or blasting the speakers out with a rasping harp solo Lee would turn the simplest available thing into a significant stage prop. The way he held and lit his chainsmoked fags, the way he covered his sweating head with a towel, the way he swigged beer from a bottle before pretending to throw it across the bar, the way he turned with his back to the audience, leaned in the bass drum and urged Figure to hit the drums 'Harder!'

At the end of each song this lurking moodiness was suddenly and confusingly dispelled as he gruffly but always politely thanked the audience before snappily announcing the title of the next tune and resuming the assault. Lee's persona was the embodiment of the so-called 'nice cop/nasty cop' routine all rolled into one. The relationship he forged with the audience was always perverse, deliberately aggressive – and the more over the

top Lee was the more the punters delighted in it. As Lee was to say 'If someone wants to have a little go, a little stare, I'll stare back.'

Wilko, meanwhile, was also on the way to becoming a *bona fide* guitar hero, his name already being spoken of alongside the likes of Townshend, Cropper and Richards. His chopping guitar style was a revelation as he stalked the stage in a series of juddering spastic lurches – and, like a magician performing some sleight-of-hand, what you saw didn't seem to bear any relation to what you heard. Huge slabs of 12-bar blues were laid down like so much crazy paving across which Wilko shimmied, strafing the audience with fragmented solos as he went.

Sparko, meanwhile, sported his Fender at chest level, shunted backwards and forwards on the stage in the manner of a naff and rather un-hip-looking showband player. Holding up the rear was the bluff-looking Figure who thumped his Gretsch kit with all the authority of the seasoned pro he always was, often sporting a double-breasted jacket, spivvy silk tie and dark glasses. He was tight. No frills. Impenetrable. Mick Farren, who was one of the first to write about the band in the *NME*, famously wrote 'They have the kind of look that makes it possible to believe that they came together in jail or in a singularly unpleasant section of the army.'

By early 1974, as the Feelgoods set about dismantling London, people were starting to be turned away from gigs. Figure recalls the surprise they got when they first arrived outside the

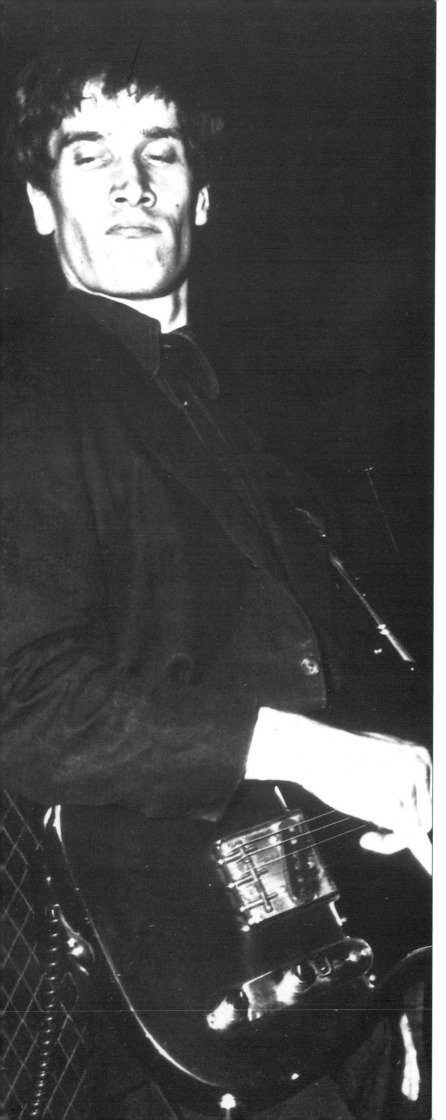

Kensington for a free Sunday lunchtime session and discovered that there was a queue that already stretched round the block.

They were getting the kind of press coverage most bands would sell their gear for, yet the band remained philosophical with a basic 'if it all ends tomorrow we'll be happy' attitude they never really lost. For perhaps the first time, though, they began to let themselves think that something bigger could actually materialise out all this excitement and that all the hard work could somehow pay off.

They'd acquired an agent in the form of Paul Conroy and Nigel Kerr at the Charisma Agency and work was flooding in. The set still comprised R&B standards ranging from Chuck Berry through to Leiber and Stoller, with a dash of the Pirates in the form of 'Hungry For Love' which Wilko sang.

Among those starting to take notice was Bob Harris, softly-spoken DJ and presenter of the thinking man's rock programme *The Old Grey Whistle Test* who, having seen the band live, had already invited the Feelgoods onto his radio show to record a session. This acted as a spur to Wilko to write some original material for the band to play. 'I think we did "She Does It Right", and I seem to recall writing it the night before. I realised that if something was going to happen we were going to need original material and so it was a matter of getting the confidence to start doing it, cos I really dig the old R&B stuff and you think, well, I can't write that good.'

As it transpired, Bob was also interested in signing the band on a development deal to manage and oversee the band's future career path. The Feelgoods invited him to Canvey to talk about the proposition further and, keen to impress him, Chris Fenwick 'borrowed' his Dad's house for the day which conveniently still had the old man's Mercedes parked in the drive. It was to this house that Harris turned up to witness an overtly stage-managed image of the Feelgoods sitting pretty.

The deal on offer, however, really seemed pointless. They didn't need another tier of fixers and arrangers with everyone taking their cut – after all they already had a manager in Chris. What was wanted was a direct signing to an established label. Other, similar conversations were to take place in the following months before a front-runner emerged in the form of United Artists.

CHEQUE BOOK

5

The London offices of United Artists Records were located in Mortimer Street above its parent company, United Artist Films. Occupying the A&R office was one Andrew Lauder, who through various successful signings such as the Groundhogs, Hawkwind and Brinsley Schwarz was rapidly gaining a reputation as the best pair of ears in London. In coming years he was to sign such notable acts as the Stranglers and the Buzzcocks, all of which conspired to make United Artists one of the most prestigious labels in England.

Lauder had first heard about the Feelgoods through Nick Lowe, at the time playing in UA band Brinsley Schwarz managed by Dai Davies. Nick was already aware of Lauder's great love of music from the great British beat boom of the early 1960s which had spawned such acts as the Paramounts, the Merseybeats and, of course, the Pirates. Andrew had recently completed a compilation LP of early Merseybeat records to put out on UA, and the Feelgoods, Lowe surmised, would be just up his street.

'They were so much better than a lot of the other groups who were around,' Lowe recalls. 'The pub-rock scene had in many ways become a bit cosy and they were anything but. They looked great, they sounded great, they had these great names they'd given themselves... At the time, there were plenty of horrible versions of "Bye Bye Johnny" and "Route 66" going about – but they weren't played like the Feelgoods played them.'

Suitably enthused, Lauder went along to see them and was immediately smitten. Yet the fact remained that a back-to-basics R&B band wasn't exactly the hippest most commercial sound around. 'It was obviously against the run of play,' Andrew recalls, 'but at that point we had enough going on at UA to be able to say "sod it, let's do it. We like it, it's a great band, let's go for it."'

Once the ink had dried and the Feelgoods were part of the UA clan, they embarked on their first proper national tour as support act for Brinsley Schwarz and Dave Edmunds on the suitably named New Favourites Tour of June-July 1974. While the band got a taste of the motorway, manager Fenwick was quickly adjusting to the band's new status as a signed act. A small advance enabled them to buy a tour bus complete with sleeping and cooking facilities, along with some new band equipment.

The year ended with a few incongruous dates supporting United Artists stablemates Hawkwind during which the far-out freaks who came to turn on, tune in and drop out to their psychedelic favourites pelted the distinctly straight-looking Feelgoods with coins. It was cash they thrived on.

Back down on Canvey, Chris Fenwick was getting organised. His builder father had given him a plot of land along the Central Wall road for his 18th birthday, and the box-shaped house built on it (quickly dubbed Feelgood House) was to become the centre of operations over the next few years. It was also to be the place where Chris and

The earliest Feelgood line-up exudes menace in a United Artists promo pic.

Lee lived during these early years as they pursued the sort of bachelor-pad lifestyle TV sitcoms have been written about. With the addition of a small rehearsal room for the band at the back, the Feelgoods were very much in business. 'We were very, very self contained,' Fenwick recalls, 'and had the advantage over other bands because of it. We weren't struggling, we had a van, we had work, we were organised.'

Chris was only too aware of the image they were putting over – an image enhanced by his dad's old Merc parked up imposingly in the small drive. 'It was an angle, we were like the last Mohicans on the Eastern River. We were a local band, a group of blokes all from the same place so if we had a journalist interested we'd invite them down, we had Feelgood House, we liked a bit of dope, we got drunk, we had a laugh – it was all very happy.'

This softly-softly public relations push was soon being translated into hard copy as music journalists of all shapes and sizes struggled manfully to define the sartorial elegance and thuggish charm of the Feelgoods, not to mention the bleak rundown environment from which they'd so spectacularly sprung. Visually the band looked great both on and off stage and so the resulting spreads were always well covered with some great hard-edged black and white photographs. With the touring schedule ever more ambitious, the word was gradually spreading.

The pressure was now on to capture the Feelgoods' bare-boned sound on vinyl – and for Andrew Lauder, Vic Maile was the only person for the job. An experienced engineer who'd cut his teeth working on the Pye mobile, Maile's impressive list of live credits ran from the Who's 'Live At Leeds' through to Hawkwind and the 'Greasy Truckers' project which had been recorded at the Roundhouse in London. For Andrew Lauder, therefore, Maile was *the* live engineer – and, as the band wanted to more or less record that way in the studio, he seemed the natural choice as producer of the Feelgoods' debut album.

As Figure recalls, 'Vic was someone who would stick up for what he felt should be on the record and the sound, but also someone who would be prepared to talk to you and compromise on certain issues.' Hitting the nail on the head, Lauder just says 'He was a beat-group kind of guy. I knew I wasn't going to sit down and have to explain it to him.'

Over a ten-day period spaced out between late August and November, Dr Feelgood travelled to Rockfield Studios in Wales and Jackson's Studio in Rickmansworth to record their much anticipated debut LP. At the forefront of everyone's minds was the nagging question which was to hound the band throughout their recording career – would it sound as good as live?

In an effort not to compromise their hard-boiled sound, it was agreed that the band should to all intents and purposes record the LP live in the studio with minimal overdubs. This approach was one that Wilko in particular wanted to pursue. He, more than the others, had developed some sense of what he wanted and how he wanted to achieve it.

Inevitably, putting such raw recruits in with a seasoned professional wasn't going to be a smooth ride. Wilko: 'Vic wanted to do it traditionally with bass and drums first, dubbing this on and then that on, I didn't know much about recording, but I didn't really like that idea and I had a bit of a ruck with him. I wanted to do it as straightforwardly as possible.'

Even Figure had at first been perplexed by the recording process as Vic had asked him to remove all the bottom skins and rims from his beloved Gretsch drumkit to enable them to be miked up properly.

Inexperience aside, the band laid down an impressive calling card including many Wilko Johnson originals which the band already played in the set. Numbers like 'Roxette', 'She Does it Right' and 'Keep It Out Of Sight' perfectly reflected the disaffected Feelgood urban image and sat comfortably next to a well-chosen selection of covers.

'Cheque Book' was borrowed from Mickey Jupp's much-loved 'Red Boot' LP, while Wilko's hero Mick Green was given a nod with the instrumental track 'Oyeh!'. These studio recordings were supplemented by the inclusion of 'Bonie Moronie/Tequila', a two-song live workout recorded earlier in the year at Dingwalls in Camden Town.

It was when the record was mixed by Maile at Pye studios in London that the most controversial aspect of the LP emerged – it was to be mixed and pressed up in mono. Wilko recalls how they arrived at this decision: 'When we were mixing it we were doing it in stereo and I was ending upon one side with Sparko on the other. It didn't sound cohesive, and a lot of the mixes just sounded better if everything was placed in the middle. Some tracks were in mono, and so we thought you'd lose less by doing it all like that.'

The idea that this was all part of some retro 'back to mono' campaign is totally dismissed by Wilko: 'I remember saying to Andrew Lauder don't write "mono" on the sleeve because it doesn't matter, nobody will know. There wasn't anything behind it, we were just trying to make the band sound right. I didn't want it to be like that art-school vibe where you're striking poses about being retrograde. That wasn't what we were doing. We were doing something that was real…'

Allied to the music was the all-important visual presentation of the band. Wilko had already thought of the title for the LP – 'Down By The Jetty'. Originally the idea had been to have a full-colour shot of the band pictured down at Canvey on the Sea Wall with the glowing refineries providing a suitably dramatic backdrop. With this, in mind several sets of pictures were taken. One morning the photographer got the band up early and blasted off a few rolls of black and white film. Thanks to the previous night's gig the quartet both looked and felt distinctly liverish as they huddled up in their suits and tried to keep warm as the sea breeze whipped across the Estuary.

It was only when Wilko later saw these more casual and less posed shots that he became enthused. 'It looked like those stills that you used to get outside a cinema, stills in which it looked like something was happening although you couldn't quite say what.' With a definite nod and a wink to the covers of both the MC5's LP 'Back In The USA' and the J Geils Band's first LP, 'Down By The Jetty' was dressed up and ready to go.

Back at United Artists, the 16-man sales force was gearing up to hit the record shops across the country. But when Chris Fenwick was called into the sales chief's office to discuss the forthcoming promotion, he was told the mono tag meant 'you might as well cut your record sales in half. My salesmen have got to sell this and it's not what people want to hear.'

Conversely, Andrew Lauder recalls the mounting excitement he had about the whole project: 'I was pretty fired up about it by that time. Everyone was saying to me you can't put out a record in mono, you can't put it out in a black and white sleeve… It became perverse in the end because you'd say that's *exactly* why we're going to do it because it really was so different from everything else.'

Top: Breakdown on the A13.

Above: The first album sleeve. Compare this image with the original (colour) cover picture on the following page.

When 'Down By The Jetty' was released in January 1975 *NME* doyen Nick Kent seized on the reference points with relish. 'Here is a band,' he crowed, 'who on anything approaching a good night can muster a ferocity so downright devastating it grabs you by the lapels, pins you to the walls with its breath and screams out "*This is Rock and Roll*".

'The Stones had it, the MC5 had it and the Feelgoods have it within their grasp to *absolutely define* the full potency of rock and roll to crackle and spark, to push the whole godforsaken energy that powerhouses the beat to its very outer limits. *And it's not here*. Not this album. But we can wait.' Essentially, close but no cigar.

While the LP hit the high streets, the Feelgoods soon found themselves back out on the road as part of a rare experiment in inter-band and record company co-operation. Just as the Iron Horse agency had opened up the pub circuit, so Nigel Kerr and Paul Conroy at the Charisma Agency dreamt up a plan to take three up-and-coming bands round the country on the same bill. The tour would book into larger halls than any one of the bands could hope to fill on its own, offering a real leg-up as they moved out of the familiar pub/club circuit to a potentially much bigger audience.

The Naughty Rhythms Tour, featuring Dr Feelgood, Kokomo and Chilli Willi and the Red Hot Peppers, duly set off on a 25-date jaunt around the country in January and February of 1975, offering a New Year bargain at an entrance fee of just 75 pence . As there was no 'headline' act it was agreed that the order of appearance would rotate every night.

Nigel Kerr: 'Today people would be too concerned about where they were going to be billed, who was going on first. In those days all the bands were pretty friendly, everyone was in their 20s and it was a good laugh, it was like going back to those 1960s' style package tours. Paul and I were trying to give people good value, that's why we gave it a title to try and capture people's imagination.'

The tour picked up a fair bit of enthusiastic press and most of the gigs either sold out or were at least respectable. The Feelgoods' act transposed well onto larger stages where they could literally find more room to roam. Highlight of the tour was the chance to play the shabbily elegant Rainbow

Theatre, at the time London's most prestigious rock venue. Although the tour wasn't structured as a make-or-break event, winners and losers soon emerged. After the tour the Chillis decided to call it a day and Kokomo drifted off towards an American sunset which left the Feelgoods as the undeniable stars of the show.

It was during this period that the Feelgoods began to settle into a routine that was to become their *modus operandi* over the next 20 years – a live touring band who were ready, willing and able to put 250 gigs a year away without concern. The Naughty Rhythms Tour had moved the Feelgoods up a definite notch, the act was catching fire every night and because they had now had an LP with a well-played single – 'Roxette' – taken off it, word of mouth was gradually spreading around the country as it had on the London pub circuit.

Soon every medium sized hall in every town in the country would echo to the same insistent chant of 'Feelgoods! Feelgoods! Feelgoods!' Brilleaux had started to wear his trademark white suit, contrasting with Wilko's all-black ensemble. After a 30-date outing, the unwashed white cloth looked more like a crumbled chip bag which had spent the night lying under a Transit van.

The band were also gaining something of a reputation as party animals. Sparko recalls the on-tour humour that was to sustain them while they moved up and down the motorways of England and later on into Europe. 'We were very heavy drinkers and visiting journalists used to try and keep up with us. Of course, we'd had five years' practice, so we'd get people *really* drunk.'

Flushed with success, United Artists were keen to return the band to the studio and capitalise on the moment. In March 1975 'She Does It Right' had been released as a second single and the band were soon back in harness to record their second LP of songs. On this occasion the chosen venue was Olympic studios in London where again it was decided to record with as little overdubbing as possible.

Vic Maile completed some tracks and the band themselves, with engineer Doug Bennett, completed the rest. It seemed the less 'produced' they were the happier they were. As Andrew Lauder remarks, by this time the band were 'becoming better and more used to the studio: they recorded with a slightly bigger sound.'

The album again featured several Wilko Johnson classics such as 'Back In The Night' and 'Going Back Home' which Wilko had co-written with his long-time hero Mick Green… 'I got to meet Mick just around the time we got signed. I'd met him before just to get his autograph when I was a lad, and this time I went round to his place. He started to play this riff and I said fucking hell, what's that? He showed me the riff and I went home and put words to it.'

Above: Wilko meets his mentor, Mick Green.

Bottom: The Naughty Rhythms crew.

The album also featured Lee's highly un-technical but very effective slide playing, which wails throughout a cracking version of Muddy Water's 'Rolling And Tumbling'. New friend Nick Lowe co-wrote the hard-as-nails 'Because You're Mine', while track number nine was the appropriately named 'Riot In Cell Block No 9' by Leiber and Stoller – a show-stopping feature of the live act.

As Figure would tap out the ominous opening beats of rhythm on the snare Sparko, Lee and Wilko would assemble in front of the drum riser and stare out the entire hall. Wilko and Sparko, toting their guitars as if they were Thompson submachine guns, would scan the audience for potential targets, Lee between them like a brooding convict in the mould of Neville Brand cast in a hard-boiled American B Movie.

Figure would then perform a roll on his snare that was the sound of a distant machine gun going off, Wilko and Sparko joining him with the thumping opening riff which echoed round the hall. This was the cue for the manic trio to walk forward in a line-up to the front of the stage where Lee would pause for a moment before barking 'On July the second 1953, I was serving time for armed robbery.'

By the time Lee was ordering the audience to 'come out with their hands up in the air' the entire hall had its arms held up obediently in an act of compliant surrender. The whole piece was simply a great slice of ham theatre served up with

mustard that was, as Lee put it, 'definitive Feelgoods.'

The sleeve of what was to be called 'Malpractice' followed the pattern that 'Jetty' had already established. A terse black and white still depicted the band again hanging around Canvey, apparently caught in the middle of something. Lee sports his white suit while Wilko catches the camera with a subtle 'don't even think it' glance. Sparko and Figure are too preoccupied to bother.

The LP was received more enthusiastically than 'Jetty', the *NME*'s Neil Spencer opening his review by saying 'The first thing about this LP is that it doesn't make sense until you play it loud.' He went on to add with mounting enthusiasm that 'it's the cure-all album that Feelgood buffs always hoped the band would make.' He concluded a full track-by-track analysis of the LP by saying 'It could even be a hit.'

Despite the fact that Rod Stewart was the current best-seller, 'Malpractice' slipped easily into the middle of the Top 30. A single, 'Back In The Night', spread the message further afield and the band were able to headline their first proper tour in the UK which later continued as the Speeding Through Europe Tour. The band were given a rapturous reception – nowhere more so than in France, where Wilko was rapidly being elevated to the status of rock guitar god.

During the summer, the band clocked up two major festival successes, at Reading and Orange in France, which saw the band conquer the two largest audiences they had ever played in front of. In a *Melody Maker* readers' poll in September, Dr Feelgood were voted second brightest hope after Camel, while the traditional 'end of year' pictorial round-up of the best and worst of the year in the *NME* included a still shot of Lee's tatty white suit hanging up in a dressing room with the caption 'Sleeve of the Year'.

For Dr Feelgood, 1975 had been like a tornado. Not only had the band released their first two albums but they'd appeared across the UK and Europe both on stage and countless TV programmes. They'd even met up with and made friends with some unlikely allies – Led Zeppelin, whose *après* Earls Court bash they had been booked to play, and also 'Mad' Frankie Frazer, who had passed on his regards after the band had played inside Wandsworth nick. Dr Feelgood were making friends in high places and had, it seemed, well and truly arrived. Everywhere at once.

WALKING ON THE EDGE

6

s Chris Fenwick now sagely remarks with more than a small degree of hindsight, 'they always say that a sure way to fucking break up a band is to send them to the States.' Success on the scale the Feelgoods were enjoying was, it seemed, bound to have a pricetag attached to it. If 1975 had been the breakthrough year, 1976 was to prove to be, perversely, even more successful and yet their most traumatic. For if the seeds of discontent were starting to sprout within the band, 1976 would see them begin to flower.

While 'Malpractice' had been breaking all over Europe, Chris Fenwick had been turning his attentions towards America which was still a territory open to them under the terms of their UA contract. Several major American records companies had already picked up on the Feelgoods' huge European success and were actively courting the band. With this in mind, towards the end of '75, Chris had been back and forth across the Atlantic more times than he cared to remember as he was courted by the biggest names in the American recording industry –

names such as Ahmet Ertegun, the legendary head of Atlantic Records whom Chris affectionately describes as a tough negotiator with 'a real bit of old-fashioned New York bollocks'.

Bruce Lundvall and CBS emerged as front-runners and Chris soon negotiated an attractive deal – with the result that the Feelgoods, like any new band, were obliged to attend one of the many sales conferences being held in one or other American city every other day of the week. It was a time, as Nick Lowe recalls, when 'the old cocktail party was really swinging, record companies would take over a hotel get all their people in and have a great big "Ra Ra session".'

So in the January of '76 the Feelgoods got on a plane and headed for San Diego where they were due to play in front of the great and the good at CBS Records prior to a proper US tour scheduled for later in the year. Along for the ride was Nick Lowe, whose band Brinsley Schwarz had recently split, and his mate (and later manager) Jake Riviera who'd formerly managed Chilli Willi and the Red Hot Peppers. Jake was operating as tour manager with Nick Lowe to all intents and purposes a roadie. He signed in to the Rivermont Hotel under the guise of Dale Liberator, Equipment Handler.

A Feelgood greetings card, personally designed by Wilko.

Each member of the band, in their different ways, was to find America something of a culture shock. As Lee was to recall, 'I thought because Americans speak English they *are* English except that they live in another part of the world, which personally I found to be a mistake. My first reaction was that we might well have landed on Mars.'

Similarly, Figure felt 'musically a little lost. I felt more at home on the continent, really'. For Wilko, America was to prove to be a 'miserable experience'. The only person who seemed to find any thing to recommend it was Sparko – who, as Andrew Lauder recalls, visibly brightened up when it was explained to him that CBS artists had an unlimited line of credit at the bar of the Rivermont Hotel where the conference was being held. It was a courtesy he took full advantage of. Andrew Lauder vaguely recalls someone floating around the following morning in the hotel fountain: it was probably a Feelgood.

The Feelgoods in America can best be summed up with the old adage 'you can take the boys out of Canvey but you can't take Canvey out of the boys.' Standing in the blazing sunshine of downtown San Diego uniformly togged out in an assortment of cheap-looking, narrow-lapelled jackets and oddly-cut trousers helped mark the Feelgoods out as something different. As Nick Lowe recalls, they looked 'like a bunch of terribly-dressed losers in thrift-store threads. They were all rather horrified by us – which, of course, made us feel great.'

The night of the Feelgoods' debut gig in America has already gone down in the annals of rock'n'roll history. The venue was a huge ballroom where five acts were each to play a 45-minute set. While the Feelgoods were hovering edgily backstage, Nick Lowe was running around busying himself and trying to do various roadie-like things out front. It was while he was running around that he knocked over Lee's old Guild slide guitar moments before they were due to take the stage.

This incident was always blamed on a roadie, but Nick is now ready to admit to it. 'I don't know how it happened, but everyone was ready to go and I looked over at this guitar and it was in two pieces. Meanwhile out on stage this guy was already announcing the act. Lee didn't say a word: he looked at the guitar, took the set list out of his pocket, got a pencil from the other pocket and calmly crossed out the two tunes that he was going to play with slide. With that, the curtain went up and on they went.'

The Feelgoods that night characteristically left the assembled multitude open-mouthed as they set about a typical half-hour slice of onstage mayhem. The American sales force brought up on a diet of bland Adult-Oriented Rock had literally never seen or heard anything quite like it. After the explosive gig ensued another 'money no object' party which involved, among other things, CBS flying in 20 hookers from LA for the occasion. At the bash a half-cut executive cornered Wilko and said 'That was a great show Wilker...' Wilko fired back 'All our shows are great, mate. Some of them are bad, but they're all great...'

It was during this period, while they were up in LA, that another incident occurred which would later resurface as the lyrics to the band's hit single 'Milk And Alcohol'. One night the boys – Lee, Chris, Sparko, Figure, Nick Lowe and Jake Riviera – decided to catch a show at the Starwood Hotel by their long-time blues hero John Lee Hooker. At the time, Hooker wasn't exactly the revitalised act he was later to become and, having had a few drinks, turned in a desultory show with a third-rate backing band. So bad, in fact, that he sacked two hapless drummers from the stage during the course of the shambolic set. *'They got him on Milk and Alcohol.'*

The Feelgood entourage left early feeling disappointed as a much-regarded icon bit the dust. On the way across town they inadvertently jumped a red light and were quickly picked up by a black and white LAPD unit. *'Sirens were screaming all around.'* They pulled over and within seconds found themselves at gunpoint being lined up on the sidewalk with hands in the air and being ordered to 'adopt the position'.

Figure recalls one of the cops as a young-looking, nervous Puerto Rican kid 'with a bloody great big .45 in his hand' who had clearly never seen the like of the crew he currently had in his custody '...and he was really shaking, which made me feel extremely nervous.' It was at this point that Nick Lowe, who had already had a few too many drinks, dropped his hands and declared "This is all Mickey Mouse! I'm going to have a fag." Figure, still with one eye locked on the muzzle of the young cop's increasingly unsteady gun, quickly intervened. 'Don't you move Nick, stay exactly as you are.'

By this time, Chris Fenwick, whose alternative managerial motto could be 'Don't expect to be a manager without spending a night in jail', was being cuffed as one of the other cops had discovered a small bag of hash in the glove compartment of the hire car. Someone was going to jail. Chris ended up before a judge who offered him the option of attending a series of socially correct drug counselling sessions. Chris accepted the option, since his arrest would not then threaten future entry into the United States. These rehabilitation sessions were, as Chris was later to discover, virtual universities of smoke fully

attended by every would-be Cheech and Chong in LA – and highly educational!

After the San Diego outing, the band returned to England to regroup before launching a formal assault on the US market. They opened later on in the year in New York with two high-profile gigs at the Bottom Line club with the Ramones as support. In the audience were the all the 'usual suspects' from New York's glitterati, from Andy Warhol down. The real test, however, would come as the band motored west into the heart of America headlining in clubs where no-one had seen or heard of them.

At this point, the Feelgoods had everything to play for and nothing to lose. The deal in America had done them no harm at all financially and CBS were ready, willing and able to pull out all the stops in order to break the act. Meanwhile, back home in England the Feelgoods could do no wrong. The public just couldn't get enough of them and even the often cynical music press loved them too.

Everyone, it seemed, loved the Feelgoods – and if they played their cards right North America seemed set to be the next territory to fall under the spell of their thrift-shop ethic. However, growing tensions had already started to surface within the Feelgood camp which would ultimately lead to a rift opening up between Wilko and the others which was to become, by the end of the tour, about as wide as the Grand Canyon.

In the rock'n'roll cookbook a common, easy-to-follow recipe for disaster goes something like this: take one group, one tour bus, mix together liberally and put out on the road for a three-month tour. Turn heat up full, and stand well back. The previous 18 months had loaded a lot of pressure on everyone and each had handled it in their own way. As principal songwriter, Wilko found it impossible to just happily knock out songs while sitting in the back of a tour bus and booking in and out of hotels.

In the previous year he had written the lion's share of two critically acclaimed LPs and was already experiencing the age-old demand to come up with another 'sock it to me ' album of songs.

In addition, as a confirmed teetotaller Wilko was, by definition, not a member of the on-road drinking club, and so while the entourage were out partying Wilko would be often back at the hotel on his own. As Phil Mitchell, current bass player with the Feelgoods, observes of the subtle mechanisms at play in any band: 'If a gap opens up for any reason between the group and one of the members it soon becomes a chasm that can't be closed.'

Wilko himself additionally acknowledges that at the time he was feeling 'pretty fucking miserable' with the whole situation which, again, wasn't endearing him to any of the others. 'I had to come up with more songs if I was to be the songwriter, and they had to be good. It worries you in a lot of ways. I was really hard to get on with, I can understand that now, and I was pretty horrible. On the other hand, they didn't realise how freaky it was because they didn't write the songs. As far as they knew, I'd go "here's a song" like it came out of nowhere and that would be the first time they would hear it. Perhaps they didn't realise how difficult it is...'

Amazingly the shows were still sharp as ever, the slowly growing off-stage tensions only adding to the dynamics. As Nick Lowe observes, 'Things were really tense with Wilko but in a way that's often what makes a band fantastic, that on-stage tension – they don't really like each other, yet they can make this fantastic sound. You see it happen so often: Oasis are an example right now. They have a fantastic tension about them which drives people wild, and the Feelgoods definitely had that in spades. It was tense, but there was never a dull moment.'

As part of their 'make or break' campaign, CBS had come up with a few high-profile gigs as support for Kiss – a band about as far away from the music and culture of Dr Feelgood as you could get. This was pantomime American style, with space-cadet sci-fi musicians decked out in absurd costumes and make-up. Yet as incongruous as the match was, the Feelgoods were up for it. So it was that they found themselves at a hotel way down south in Mobile, Texas while Chris Fenwick went down to the football stadium to suss the gig out.

It soon became clear that the Kiss entourage weren't exactly brimming with excitement at the match – and, after being shown to some backstage public toilets when he asked to see the band's dressing rooms, Chris returned to the hotel and announced he'd blown the gigs out. Blowing out Kiss wasn't exactly going to endear the band to CBS, but they hadn't travelled halfway across

America to have the piss taken by a bunch of cartoon characters.

Afterwards the band decided to use the unexpected free days in their schedule to take in New Orleans – the perfect town for a bloke from Canvey called Brilleaux. Once again Wilko excluded himself from the 'party' by electing to stay behind and catch up with everyone later in time for the coming LA dates.

Internal problems aside, Chris Fenwick remains philosophical about the whole American exploit putting a lot of it down to different business attitudes. 'The problem with the States was that back in England we were doing two nights at Hammersmith, the Southend Kursaal, the Cambridge Corn Exchange, it was cooking. We get to the States where no one had heard of us – it was start again.'

In addition, none of the Feelgoods were particularly adept when it came to dealing with the American way of business. Chris Fenwick: 'By the mid-1970s, American musicians were much more businesslike than their English counterparts: they knew how to smarm up and schmooze, and we never had that. In the UK we had a nice cosy set-up with United Artists and suddenly in America you've got this monster on your hands. You'd meet the wrong bloke at CBS who'd say something like "Look guys what you should be doing is..." And you'd think "Don't fucking tell *me* what we should be doing..."'

Brilleaux, who thrived on the touring experience, could also get rubbed up the wrong way. 'Sometimes when you're out on the road, record companies say things about you which are not true and sometimes you say similar things which you really believe at the time. But come the night of the gig you're fucked up, it's your 14th day on the road, I haven't had a break, I'm away from home, I got all these record company people around me, I couldn't give a fucking Empress of India, I'm going home, I'm going back to my hotel room...'

In later years, Lee summed the whole America versus Dr Feelgood scenario to Larry Wallis when he said 'The Septic tanks? They don't like us and we don't like them.' Lee was, of course, talking subjectively, as he later found himself married to an American girl.

Chris Fenwick, meanwhile, also remains sanguine about the eternal 'could they have cracked America?' question when he wistfully replies 'If your auntie had balls she'd be your uncle...' This, of course, is true.

Wilko plays at Pirates with Mick Green and Johnny Spence.

GOING BACK HOME

7

Back on Canvey, a few key changes were by now taking place to the 'Oil City' empire. Chris Fenwick had traded up and moved from his first adolescent gaff, Feelgood House, to another much more impressive 1930s-styled house on the Island. The huge eight-roomed building was surrounded by a suitably improbable croquet lawn and also had, to the rear, an old corrugated Nissen hut which had originally housed a full-sized billiard table. This pile was instantly dubbed Feelgood House Two.

If Feelgood House One had been an ideal setting for a sitcom series then this place was in the ensuing years to become more like *Feelgood House – The Movie*. To ensure that the place ran smoothly a fully operational bar was installed in the living room by Sparko, and this soon attracted the name of the Cluedo Club. Here, to the routine shout of 'Get this down yer, weasel', Chris, Lee and a band of highly irregular regulars whiled away their 'off the road' periods.

The old billiard room was also easily converted by Sparko into a rehearsal room-cum-recording studio in which basic demos could be recorded. It was here that Sparko produced the classic Lew Lewis track 'Boogie On The Street' which came out later in October 1976 on newly-formed Stiff Records to universal praise. Stiff was, of course, the brainchild of two aspirant moguls: Dave Robinson and by now former Feelgood tour manger Jake Riviera.

Jake had been for some time harbouring the idea for a downhome record label that would be an antidote to the faceless 'big combo' that the music business was gradually becoming. He'd raised the finance for his first release, 'So It Goes' by Feelgood 'roadie' Nick Lowe, by casting around all his mates in the business who had the slightest whiff of money in the bank. Accordingly, Lee Brilleaux had chipped in a helpful 400 quid and the rest, as they say, is history.

In those days, it seemed if you weren't in the demo studio or the Cluedo Club then you were round the local, Admiral Jellicoe, sinking pints. Once the band had returned from America to the familiarity of Canvey, they soon found themselves under mounting pressure to deliver the next album. 'Malpractice' had been released the previous October and it was fast approaching a whole year since the band had released anything new. At this precise moment in time, however, this just wasn't going to happen.

The definitive Feelgood image, as immortalised on the 'Stupidity' sleeve.

Wilko was certainly using any and all of his available off-road time to work on new ideas but the band were still heavily committed to touring in Europe as well as a taking on a whole range of one-off TV appearances. He simply needed something which the Feelgoods just didn't have – more time.

It was from this position of weakness that a germ of an idea began to develop. As Figure recalls it: 'The United Artists sales reps were always on our backs to do a live LP and there had been this constant thing in the press about our records which were always "not quite good as live". Wilko

was struggling to write, so a live LP seemed like a good idea.'

For Andrew Lauder at United Artists, the idea seemed not only attractive but in many ways inevitable. After all, the Feelgoods were the premier live band in the country and it seemed only logical that a live album would be released at some stage in their career. Now seemed like as good a time as any.

Several live recordings of the band had, in fact, already been made by Vic Maile and the Pye mobile in the previous year when the Feelgoods were truly conquering Britain. The shows captured on tape had been at Sheffield (May 1975) and the Kursaal in Southend (November 1975). The recordings had caught the Feelgoods at their strident best, and plans were quickly laid to turn them into a live LP with the offbeat title of 'Stupidity'.

Once again the question of how far to go in remixing the tracks became a very hot issue. At the time many live LPs that were released had routinely been well doctored in the recording studio in order to iron out any blemishes. A snare-drum track could be simply re-recorded to make it sound more prominent, dodgy guitar solos could

be replayed and more applause could be dubbed on to make it all sound more exciting.

Yet Andrew Lauder felt that as far as this record was concerned the overall ambience of the tracks was an important issue. He wanted to feel that he was hearing the band as if he was right down at the front of the stage, whereas Wilko felt the opposite. He wanted to have a wider sense of the hall in which the gig was being played. Generally, Andrew felt that 'there was too much audience and that the ambience was wrong.' Wilko was sticking to his guns preferring it 'warts and all...in the end I'm eyeball to eyeball and had a big row with Andrew Lauder.'

Finally Wilko's preference prevailed and the LP was released in October along with a massive push from the United Artists sales reps who marketed the album as keenly as if it were a brand new set of songs. In addition, the first 20,000 copies contained a free single. Partly as a result of this concerted push the record slipped easily into the middle of the charts in its first week of release. By this time it seemed as if every record shop in Britain boasted a huge reproduction of the classic Lee/Wilko cover shot in their window which said everything about the band as a live draw.

The following week of 9 October the album was propelled straight towards the Number 1 spot. Typically the band first heard the news after a gig while still out on tour in southern England and, as Chris Fenwick recalls, the 'party that night was pretty severe.'

It was in effect to be the Feelgoods' crowning moment. A massive and definitive thumbs-up from every single punter in the country who had ever seen the band perform live. Now they could take a little bit of the magic home with them. It was also a tacit vote of confidence in the whole anti-rock star stance taken by the band and as expounded by Lee Brilleaux when he told Allan Jones of *Melody Maker* that 'Rock'n'roll isn't fuckin' about satin trousers and limousines and massive banks of speakers and thousands of roadies everywhere. It's about people. Human beings. They are important, the rest doesn't mean a thing.'

The LP was greeted by the press with similar open arms. Charles Shaar Murray writing in the *NME* put it simply by saying 'They finally got it right' and *Sounds* gave it a five-star review under the headline 'Woooryeeh!' For a moment, the Feelgoods had become untouchable.

Though flushed with this success, the band remained their usual bluff, approachable selves. As Chris puts it, 'If you don't expect anything it's a real bit of fun when it comes – not "it should have happened ages ago, or it should have happened on the last LP but the record company fucked it up." We used to meet so many negative people in those days that all thought they should be bigger than they were and blamed everyone from record

Lee jams with the Pirates at the New Musical Express *Christmas party, 1976.*

companies to journalists. Not so with us. With us, it was always any excuse for a party. If it was a bad day you had a party. If it was a good day you had a party. This was the sort of attitude that helped us along.'

The year ended with a crowning gig at the non-seated Hammersmith Palais during which Lee was pictured in his *de rigueur* tatty white jacket walking out onstage and carrying a giant cardboard safety pin as a wry comment on the musical revolution that was currently sweeping across Britain led by Malcolm McLaren and his four protégés…Messrs Rotten, Jones, Matlock and Cook.

Somewhat perversely, the massive success of 'Stupidity' – a release designed to take some pressure off the band – only served to pile it on again. Charles Shaar Murray's red-hot review had contained a prophetic sting in its tale when he asked 'The only worry is where do the Feelgoods go after this?' 'Stupidity' had bought some much-needed breathing space, but the fact still remained that sooner or later Wilko would be under pressure once again to come up with the next album. After hitting the Number 1 spot, anything less could be seen as a failure.

In addition America couldn't simply be ignored. CBS had released 'Malpractice' as their debut disc but had decided against 'Stupidity' as it was felt to be so uniquely English. Chris recalls that generally 'CBS had the hump with us: it wasn't quite the high-profile signing that they all thought and it wasn't kicking in.' Relations within the band remained strained, and with typical Feelgood style the camp closed ranks refusing to wash any of their dirty linen in the pages of music press. All that mattered as far as the rest of the world was concerned was that everything in the Feelgood garden was rosy, with the new LP project well in hand. In reality, that was far from the truth.

When invited to fly out at CBS's expense to yet another record-company junket in LA, Chris found himself placed next to a genial 50-something black guy who turned out to be Bert de Coteaux, a CBS house producer who had produced such American R&B acts as Ben E King and the Manhattans. As Chris recalls of their first casual meeting, 'I said how do you do, I'm Chris Fenwick, manager of Dr Feelgood, and he said "I *love* Dr Feelgood" – they always say that even though they've never heard of you.'

While hanging out in LA, Chris put the current situation into some sort of perspective. He concluded that overall as manager of the band he was in something of a weak position. 'Malpractice' had been released and the band had received a contractual payment for it. CBS had then declined 'Stupidity' – and yet, in a gesture of good faith, had still paid for it under their contractual obligation.

Now with a prospective third LP in the offing, delivery of which was worth what Chris euphemistically refers to as 'a significant piece of action', he felt that they had to ensure it worked on both sides of the Atlantic. With the band generally falling out among themselves Chris had a delicate situation on his hands. He began to think of Bert de Coteaux as a prospective producer, if only on the basis that 'CBS will love it, they'll have some control and it will have an American link. If it works, politically I'm in.'

CBS, still keen to break the band, were naturally delighted with the idea. Back in England, Andrew Lauder felt that the idea was 'an intriguing match'. Chris put it to Lee, Sparko and Figure first before taking Lee along to put it to Wilko, who by this time had symbolically moved off Canvey. They approached him with a degree of apprehension and were, according to Wilko, surprised at his enthusiasm. Brilleaux himself said that 'In a way we wanted to prove something, we had never worked with a sophisticated producer before and I think we wanted to do it as an experiment.'

It was agreed that both Lee and Wilko would fly out to meet de Coteaux at yet another CBS convention, this time in Atlanta. As Wilko recalls 'I was all for it. Lee and I went out to the convention to meet Bert and during those few days together we were trying to mend our relationship and tried hard to be friends again.' The meeting with de Coteaux was a success, with Lee and Wilko warming to the genial pro who had recorded more LPs than they had eaten hot motorway breakfasts.

Having proved their effectiveness as a hard-as-nails R&B band, the next studio LP had, in ways which were yet to be defined, to be a departure from what had gone before. 'Stupidity' had effectively drawn something of a line under the Feelgoods' act and de Coteaux had the potential to take the band into a slightly different and perhaps more commercially accessible area. Bruce Lundvall, the president of CBS who had actually signed the band, enthused that 'with this one we're going to break it open.'

The studio chosen was the familiar Rockfield where the band had recorded 'Jetty'. Here the band could concentrate on the matter in hand, with the occasional diversion to one of several very convivial nearby hostelries. As recording approached, the pressure on Wilko built up as he desperately worked to prepare songs to take down to Wales. 'I was writing songs right up until the sessions started. I was writing at Rockfield: I would stay awake for two or three days writing and writing, doing songs and crashing out.'

In addition personal relationships were still very fragile, with the 'you and us' vibe still very much in the air. Wilko: 'They were all going down

to the pub talking about me, and it all got like that.' Within 24 hours of the opening sessions de Coteaux pulled Fenwick aside and put his cards straight on the table by saying 'They ain't got any songs here, man.' Chris explained the internal rift in the group which was by now beginning to surface. Bert rolled up his sleeves and said 'I've been here before – we'll cruise this.' As Chris puts it in describing this formidable character, 'You don't argue with Bert de Coteaux, this isn't some lightweight...'

The new material that Wilko had written was slowly being worked on and recorded, additional songs being virtually written in the studio. All the time de Coteaux was leading from the front and pushing hard in an effort to keep the creative ball

rolling. Finally, as the end of the sessions approached, it was painfully clear that the band still didn't have a complete album laid down on tape. The dilemma prompted the suggestion of covering a song written by Canvey Island harp player Lew Lewis titled 'Lucky Seven'. This then became the catalyst for the disagreements which had lain dormant for some 18 months to erupt.

As Wilko explains, there was more to it than simply an argument about an individual song. 'I had written this other song ages before which I never intended the Feelgoods to record. Tim Hinkley, who had come down to play keyboards on the LP, had heard it and suggested that we try it. I said I'd not really thought about it. Anyway, I re-arranged it a bit, and we'd laid down a backing

Lew Lewis, whose song 'Lucky Seven' unwittingly proved a sticking point in the recording of 'Sneakin' Suspicion'.

track, and one evening Lee came to my room and said "Wilk, I can't do that song, I just can't." So I said "OK if you can't you can't, that's the end of it."'

Bert, meanwhile, was still pushing everyone to come up with a full album's worth of tracks. Unlike Lee, he was very enthusiastic about the track and encouraged the reluctant singer to give the song another try – even though, according to Wilko, it simply wasn't suited to Lee's voice and style of delivery. As such, and supported by Wilko, it was decided finally to drop the song. When 'Lucky Seven' was subsequently suggested, Wilko voiced his particular objections to the idea. He simply didn't like the track and felt that his wishes should be respected in the same way as he'd respected Lee's over the earlier song.

However, with time running out, and with the rest of the band set on it, battle lines were drawn. By next morning, Wilko was effectively estranged from the group with nobody in a mood to woo him back – the situation was now out in the open and totally unworkable. As Wilko puts it: 'It wasn't about the song – it was the principle and the fact that we couldn't stand each other by then.'

Bert de Coteaux departed for the States with the masters. In just over a week he'd mixed the album and played it to CBS who really liked the smoother, more produced sound. Encouraged by this, Chris decided to fly out to New York immediately with Lee and level with CBS. Occupying Chris's thoughts at the time was the simple fact that he had a band on his hands that was potentially about to implode and who had only just delivered the first LP that their American record company had genuinely liked.

Once they'd accepted it, Dr Feelgood were due another 'very substantial piece of action'. It was therefore essential that CBS didn't get to hear upsetting rumours about the band and start to get cold feet about the whole deal.

With this in mind, Lee and Chris headed to New York to secure their position and to reassure CBS that, whatever the situation Dr Feelgood were currently in, they were at the same time very much still in business. At CBS, Bruce Lundvall glowed with enthusiasm. Chris and Lee sat in front him waiting to upset his applecart.

'We then say "We've got a problem: Wilko's left." He says "You can patch it up." We say "No we can't. It's become unworkable…however, we are still consolidated, we have gigs booked and we will find a replacement."'

Lundvall was so delighted with the new LP and happy enough with Lee and Chris's assurances. And so it was that the boys walked out of CBS with heads held high, everyone feeling secure and safe in the knowledge that all monies due on delivery of the album would be paid. The band were still in business…but only just.

NINETY NINE AND A HALF (WON'T DO)

8

Back in England, Chris Fenwick's immediate concern was to get the band back on the road as soon as possible. Any hopes that Wilko could be somehow reinstated had totally evaporated by this time. The press had already picked up on the story. The *NME* of 9 April 1977 ran a storyline with the headline 'Sacked – or did he sack himself?' As Fenwick recalls it, the mood in the band was pragmatic: 'Shall we keep going? Yes, let's try.

'It may not work, everyone is saying "it won't work without Wilko…" All right, let it not work! Additionally my thing was don't let them (Lee, Figure and Sparko) sit around for too long and freak out. I said to them we have shows booked in three weeks in Munich, so get up there with another guitarist and I don't care who the fuck it is…'

As Lee was later to recall, despite the trauma it was 'something of a relief, really, because there had been a lot of tension in the band. I thought it could be the end, but if it is then so what? We've had a good innings. In a way it was all quite exciting because after about two days we decided that we weren't going to quit – so we set about the impossible task, or so we thought at the time, of replacing Wilko.'

While the band applied themselves to the job in hand, Chris finally secured the contractual payments due from CBS and sat down with Wilko's lawyers to thrash out a divorce settlement that was as mutually amicable as possible under the circumstances. As Chris recalls it, at the end of the day they 'shook hands, there was a resentment but that was it.'

New boy John 'Gypie' Mayo (standing, centre) adds a distinctive new hairstyle to the band's collection.

To cover the immediate European gigs that were contractually in the frame, the band hired seasoned pro Henry McCullough, the guitarist who had played with such diverse talents as Joe Cocker's Grease Band, Paul McCartney's Wings and Hinkley's Heroes with former Hendrix drummer Mitch Mitchell. This got the band straight out and onto a stage again. By the time they returned from Europe, a name had cropped up of someone who could possibly handle the position on a full-time basis. The name was John Mayo.

It had been the American singer George Hatcher who made the connection. Hatcher, a man Chris calls a 'barmy hellraiser', fronted his own boogie band which had supported the Feelgoods on several occasions back in 1975. He'd met Mayo, a self-confessed Peter Green fan, through mutual musical acquaintances and had remembered the name. By the time Lee had been given his number, John was living in a sub-let council flat in Harlow with no regular gig to speak of.

Mayo recalls picking up the *NME* at the time, reading that Wilko had left and thinking, 'Well, no more Wilko, no more Feelgoods.' A couple of weeks later, he found himself down on Canvey Island staying at Feelgood House and being broken in as the new boy. It was, as John recalls it, 'a mindfucker…'

Straight away, Lee had been impressed with John's particular picking technique which had immediately boosted the band's overall sound. 'He's got an amazing way of playing: he can play the bass notes and make rhythm while his other fingers pick out the tune, so a real lot is going on in his department to fill the sound out a little. In the same way that Wilko had that chopping style, John's way is different but it does the same job.'

The first change John underwent when he was confirmed as the new member was that he quickly gained a new moniker. 'Everyone had a nickname,' explained the new boy – and besides 'apart from Lee we were all called John. At the time of joining I remember I had a series of minor ailments, like bad teeth, a perpetual cold, a touch of gastroenteritis, and Lee just said one day "You've always got something wrong with you, you've always got the gyp." The name stuck.'

The new-look band's first gig was a low-key introductory effort at a disco bar on Canvey called Bardot's. The band's equipment was set up at audience level on the floor and while an expectant crowd packed into see the new boy at work Lee calmly racked up at the pool table and relaxed into the evening. Naturally, as the new gun in town, Gypie felt somewhat apprehensive. This, after all, was the biggest group he had ever played with and things were suddenly moving very quickly for him.

'It wasn't easy. The musical side of it I didn't have a problem with, really: it was, after all, fast and frantic good-time music. Onstage the ghost of Wilko was still there as quite a few people at later gigs still shouted for him, but there was a united feeling which the band put across. I'm not the showman that Wilko is, he's a one-off.'

With Lee taking charge of the stage and urging him forwards – often physically – into the glare of the disco stagelights to display his talents, Gypie was effectively baptised as the new Feelgood. Any early thoughts of perhaps adding a keyboard player to fill the sound out soon fell by the wayside as Mayo slotted in both musically and socially beyond anyone's expectations. As Chris says, 'He was an agreeable bloke, he liked to drink, he liked a bit of dope, he liked women – which we all did.'

Dr Feelgood were soon back on the road departing almost immediately for a European jaunt into Holland before returning to play on home territory. Figure recalls that 'At the time we had a hell-for-leather attitude of "let's play" at every opportunity because the more exposure we had the more the ball would keep rolling.' Musing about the new line-up in the *NME*, Tony Parsons wrote 'All I know is that a short while ago the Feelgoods without Wilko would have been unthinkable. I wish John Mayo the best of luck, I think he's going to need it.'

If Bardot's had been his introduction to the public, the venue chosen for the Gypie's formal UK debut – Hammersmith Odeon – was bound to test anyone. On the night it was to be just another successful gig with Gypie taking to the giant stage with alacrity. Musically and personally, each passing gig saw him beginning to settle in and understand a little more about where the band was coming from.

'I'd never met anyone like these guys before. To be honest they weren't like the musicians I'd been used to, apart from Figure perhaps. Lee and Sparko thought of it more as "this music lark". When you're on tour you tend to talk a lot about music: with the Feelgoods it would be a lot of other things, much of it X-rated, real lads' stuff, very funny. I'd never met such a funny bunch of people before.'

The next few years was to prove to be a most productive and highly successful era, the Feelgoods extending their theatre of operations right round the world to take in Australia, New Zealand and Japan and were never off the road for any length of time. With the departure of his original foil, Lee assumed the role of frontman and bandleader and his onstage persona developed accordingly.

Gypie Mayo: 'The emphasis had shifted: there was a lot more on Lee's shoulders, but he was the

sort of person who could rise to a challenge. He wasn't going to back off and I think it brought out his more flamboyant side.'

The release of 'Sneakin' Suspicion' in May 1977 put the Feelgoods in the incongruous position of promoting an LP which had effectively nothing do with their present or future plans. Without Wilko it was a different band entirely, and reviews were mixed. Charles Shaar Murray's review appeared under the depressing headline 'Is there a doctor in the house?' In it, he mused about the soundness of using a producer like Bert de Coteaux for a band 'who had never been produced before.' The track 'Walking On The Edge' was held up as the nearest in spirit to the old band. He concluded 'What a senseless waste of human life.' Wilko, who didn't hear the album until it was mixed and released, dismissively sums it up – 'Slick, although it's not slickly played.'

The departure of Wilko also prompted some changes in the set list, since certain key show-stoppers like 'Riot In Cell Block No 9' wouldn't work with the new line-up. As Lee put it, 'That number was very much Wilko's, even though I was singing, with the machine-gun guitars and everything. There would be no point in playing it, it would be an insult to Wilko really and it just wouldn't serve any purpose.'

On the road once again, the band tore into a UK tour with renewed vigour and with Gypie sporting a distinctive black waistcoat on top of a black and white striped top it seemed he was unconsciously evoking the spirit of the Pirates. As his confidence grew and his stage presence became further established, he started to win over some old friends. *NME* journalist Nick Kent was very enthusiastic as he described Gypie as 'a real find, a nice dog-eared bully boy...the best thing that could have happened to the Feelgoods.'

With the traumas of the early part of the year behind them and with a new critical acceptance achieved, Chris Fenwick recalls a much more casual and relaxed approach starting to operate within the band. 'I was feeling a bit bulletproof, I started to enjoy things again.'

If Gypie had any lingering doubts about his role in the group, it was to centre around the perennial question that was to dog the Feelgoods over the coming the years: 'Where's the new material coming from?' Neither Lee, Sparko or Figure wrote songs in any active sense. They were always ready, willing and able to supply a line here or a riff there, but essentially Dr Feelgood found themselves a band without a songwriter. Gypie himself recalls that, for him, 'writing came out of necessity. I'm not a songwriter. I don't have that particular muse. I can come up with musical ideas, but I don't sit down and write songs.'

Stripe me! Gypie the guitarist gets piratical as Lee ponders.

With United Artists keen to have a new album from the new line-up, Gypie was going to have to learn fast. As manager, Chris felt duty bound to lay down the law. 'Don't make a fucking drama out of it and don't turn up at the studio unprepared. You can't pull that one again – ever. So have a good rehearsal period, make sure you've got enough material and learn by your mistakes.'

With this in mind, the band cast about for a producer who could capture the raw energy of the band without compromising their rough-edged approach. Andrew Lauder suggested Nick Lowe, who was by this time starting to make a name for himself as producer of Elvis Costello and the Dammed and was referred to in the press as 'Basher' after his self-proclaimed, no-nonsense, 'bash it all down and tart it up later' approach to recording. Lauder thought it a match made in heaven.

Lowe had travelled down to Feelgood House to spend a few days listening to the proposed selection of songs and also to knock some other looser material into shape. On the eve of his return to London, Mayo recalls Nick quietly explaining to him that, once in the studio, he would expect him to supply the musical direction. Gypie: 'I think he realised that Lee was more of a showman, he wasn't a musical singer. He did become more musical, but back then he was a barker – a very good one.'

Lee himself was fully prepared for the Lowe approach to recording. 'Nick looks at everything like it should be a pop tune. He reckons that there should be an introduction, a first verse that opens up the story, like every song should have a story, then with every verse something else should happen and it should all last two or three minutes and then it should go out. That's his approach and it fits in with us fine.'

The proposed studio was a suitably low-key and unfussy eight-track called Pathway, a regular Lowe haunt which he felt would suit the band to a tee. Along with original material, the band had also made a selection of some suitable covers to record, taken from such diverse talents as Johnny Guitar Watson to Isaac Hayes. Gypie contributed the easy-

Below: Now a successful producer, Nick Lowe was on the way up when he answered the Feelgoods' call.

Opposite: The Feelgoods display their new Prisoner *image.*

listening instrumental 'Hi-Rise', Lowe threw into the pot his own very punchy 'That's It I Quit' and the band began to record. Nick, however, always felt generally 'disappointed with the job that I did because they were such a great live band who weren't very good in the studio.'

More directly, Lowe feels that the band couldn't stand the tedious rigours of the recording process in which every beat and inflection is held up for scrutiny. He recalls that, to get into a suitable vibe to lay a track down, everyone would naturally end up drinking too much 'in order to get that excitement of playing live in front of a crowd feeling.' As the sessions drew to an end, material was still being hurriedly cobbled together in the studio, with Gypie throwing out riffs and lyrics coming in from all and sundry in one final effort.

Pink Fairy Larry Wallis came up with one of the new album's best songs.

Finally, still short of both inspiration and songs, a call was put into Stiff Records where Larry Wallis of the Pink Fairies was hanging out: 'Nick Lowe was in the studio and freaking out. As producer, it was his job to get some songs together – and at the time they were going a little white around the gills because they didn't have enough material.'

Wallis rashly agreed over the phone to come down to the studio the following morning with a suitable song. Always operating best under pressure, he went home that night and wrote 'As Long As The Price Is Right', conceived from scratch as a perfect slice of Feelgood imagery. The following morning Larry turned up at the studio and presented his handiwork to Nick Lowe for perusal. The last verse of the song as written went 'Beautiful Lady, I found the hotel Queen, she asked me for a hand with the zip on her dress, I said oui babe, that's French for yes.'

As Larry recalls, 'Nick took one look at that and said Brilleaux will never in a million years sing the line "Beautiful Lady…"' The line was changed to the more general 'Looking for a good time…' and the track was recorded, eventually becoming one of the best songs on the album that was soon being referred to as 'Be Seeing You'.

This catchphrase title was a direct reference to the popular 1960s' cult television programme *The Prisoner* starring Patrick MacGoohan, which was at the time enjoying something of a rebirth on English television. In the same way that *Hawaii-Five-O* some years earlier had supplied much of the Feelgood humour, now it was *The Prisoner*, with both Lee and Sparko full of the absurd lingo which the programme was known. By the time the LP was delivered to the record company, *The Prisoner* theme seemed like a good gag to hang the whole project on. After all, as Chris puts it, it was 'a bit of a crack, either you come up with an idea or the record company will. *The Prisoner* just happened to be there at the time.'

Consequently, the boys togged themselves up in the distinctive fluted jackets and university scarves of the inhabitants of the mysterious village, had a few pictures taken down on the sea wall and all of a sudden a marketing concept had been born. The cover of the LP, however, remained firmly rooted on Canvey, a snap of the band being taken in their favourite watering hole, the Admiral Jellicoe.

Mick Farren of the *NME* remained unconvinced about it all. His review went under the headline 'Prisoners of Rock?' He offered up the Larry Wallis track as the best cut on the record and concluded somewhat gloomily 'There is a conservatism creeping into the Feelgood work. (Conservatism with a small "c".)'

If the studio was, as Nick Lowe attests, 'not their natural territory', live was the same rock-steady story. In September and October, the band headed out on a full UK tour with Mink De Ville in support. The set had grown away from the earlier beat-boom sound as pioneered by Wilko and was by

now a fuller, more rounded, bluesier sound. The band remained untroubled by any lukewarm reviews of their recorded output, preferring to put everything they had onto the live stage.

Settling into life on the road became something of an adventure. Lee began to develop an interest in good food washed down with even better wine. Touring in the UK was consequently guided up and down the motorway network by a handy guide which Russell Harty had penned called *Just Off The Motorway*. With this in one hand and the steering wheel in the other, Lee would navigate the band away from the hell of motorway services and towards all manner of cosy country pubs and well-regarded restaurants. On the continent, Lee soon picked up on the Michelin guides and moved around every country in Europe via some of the finest and most famous restaurants and bars he could find. It was through this process of first-hand experience that Lee, in the ensuing years, was to become a connoisseur who would travel considerable distances to experience a particular dish or bottle of wine.

Larry Wallis recalls a conversation with Lee in which he said 'You are a bit of a gourmet.' Lee denied the accusation outright, preferring to use the similar word ' Gourmand' which is in fact a glutton. It was generally agreed between them that, whatever the choice of word, Brilleaux was a good old-fashioned 'trencherman'…

Where Lee led Figure was only too keen to follow, while Sparko was content in the role of 'clown prince' with many a dry quip enlivening the tour bus routine. His most audacious gag came in the form of an elaborate 'set piece' of which Figure was the intended target. Booking into a hotel somewhere in the north of England, everyone had remarked about its similarity to *The Munsters* or *The Addams Family*.

Keen to exploit the implications, Sparko decided to rig up Figure's room using a few yards of handy fishing tackle while he was out. Along with Dean, the tour manager, he attached several lengths of the invisible fishing line to various drawers, wardrobe doors and duvet covers, and laid the ends under the rugs and out under the door. Later that night while Figure was relaxing on his bed, Walkman on head and spliff in hand, Sparko went to work. He gave each single line a tug, a wardrobe door creaked open. Another tug and a drawer slid open. Figure had by now caught sight of these unexplained movements and was already rushing towards his own internal panic button. Finally one last tug of another line sent the duvet flying off the bed, with Figure by now in hot pursuit of the fleeing Sparko.

Gypie Mayo generally recalls that being out on the road with the Feelgoods in those days was often almost like being on tour in some kind English Gentlemen's club which had its roots way back somewhere in the 18th Century. 'Lee was quite influential and probably the strongest personality in the group. There were two sides to Lee: the wild party-going animal and the very well-read, intelligent, aware person who enjoyed history and particularly the rakes of Hogarth's London.'

As a consequence of this interest, and to further add a bit of mischief to life on the road, Lee instigated a few short-lived band fashions. One of of these concerned that most gentlemanly and very 18th Century product – snuff, which the band soon wittily dubbed 'Sidney' to distinguish it from its near relation 'Charlie'. As a consequence of this fad, snuff, snuff boxes and snuff handkerchiefs were purchased from a tobacconists in the Charing Cross Road and for a while the filthy habit was pursued. Gypie recalls the whole historical vibe eventually snowballing, Lee suggesting the addition of silver hipflasks and further talk of silver-topped walking canes.

The band had re-signed with United Artists and were due to go back into the studio to record the next LP with house producer Martin Rushent, who'd already recorded such high-profile acts as the Stranglers and the Buzzcocks. Eden Studios in London was the venue as 'Every Kind Of Vice' and Mickey Jupp's 'Down At The Doctors' were committed to tape. However Rushent fell ill with hepatitis before the LP could be completed and, with studio time booked, the band urgently needed a producer to step into the breech.

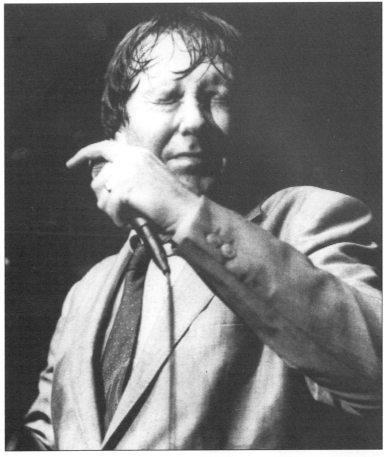

American Richard Gottehrer, Seymour Stein's partner in the Sire label, was in town at the time. A well regarded producer, he'd been a part of the writing/production team emerging from 1960s garage band the Strangeloves which had a sizeable hit with the song 'Night Time'. The team had subsequently gone on to work with the McCoys, producing the bubblegum chart-topper 'Hang On Sloopy'. More recently, he'd produced albums by the New York cult favourites Richard Hell and the Voidoids and alternative pop sensations Blondie. All in all, it was an interesting match.

Chris Fenwick had met Gottehrer and Stein when he had first gone to the States to seek a deal: he introduced the band to Gottehrer and his position as replacement producer was confirmed. The ensuing recording process was to follow much the same path as 'Be Seeing You', Gypie having brought along a few outline ideas which had been demoed in the studio at Feelgood House to augment the usual list of suggested covers. This time, the band had the aforementioned 'Down At The Doctors', while Gottehrer suggested a cover of his own 'Night Time'.

Among Gypie's less fully-formed ideas which would need further knocking into shape was a chunky-sounding riff he'd first played to Lee in a dressing room in Holland. The band laid it down as an instrumental backing track and, again finding themselves short of a lyric, phoned up Nick Lowe who was, as he recalls, at the time sitting at home watching the television. 'They phoned me up and said we've got this great backing track. Lee has something of a tune which he had been singing over it, but no lyrics. So I just went down to the studio and did it.'

The song Nick conjured up in response to the riff was 'Milk And Alcohol', all about the night he and the band had been hauled over by the LAPD after the Hooker gig. Nick similarly put lyrics to another backing track and 'It Wasn't Me' was born. The resulting album was titled 'Private Practice' and revealed the Feelgoods at their tough-talking best. The cover featured an improbable 'lookalike' of the Dr Feelgood logo along with a few casual-looking snaps of the band standing around a doorway in Harley Street, the presence of 'Steve's Cabs' maintaining the necessary link with Canvey.

Hot Press headlined their review 'The Doctor's getting Classy' and they were. Gottehrer had recorded the band with a hard-boiled and muscular swagger that wasn't a million miles away from the J Geils Band of the early 1970s which they had once so admired. It was a punchily-produced sound which didn't compromise the overall vibe of the band.

To stir up a bit of UK press interest for the new album, Chris persuaded United Artists to let him throw a launch party down on Canvey. A plush recording studio in London would otherwise have been booked, at considerable expense, and all manner of journalists wheeled in to have a glass of wine while the new LP was blasted out of huge state-of-the-art speakers. Chris felt he could do a lot better for the money, and dreamt up something he felt sure would stick in journalists' minds.

Given the green light from UA, he booked the Admiral Jellicoe on Canvey and bussed in London's finest writers for a real man's day out. This beer and lager fest was further enhanced by the appearance of several very brassy-looking strippers who proceeded to give a display of topless snooker. The resulting pictures of the 'do' suggest you probably had to have been there to fully appreciate the sporting innovation. Aesthetics aside, the launch had the desired effect as the following week Chris recalls 'we got album of the week in three papers, which just goes to show...'

The hastily penned 'Milk And Alcohol' was the obvious choice as a single and was released in January 1979, pressed on different coloured vinyls and put in a sleeve based on a bottle of the alcoholic tipple Kahlua. The record started to pick up airplays and quickly entered the UK Top 30. Suddenly, Dr Feelgood were in demand again, appearing on *Top Of The Pops* and a whole string of European TV shows. Bolstered by this success, the live work went up a few notches and the band enjoyed their most successful year since 'Stupidity' three years previously.

With Michelin guides in hand, Brilleaux directed the band across Europe, ending the year

The launch party for 'Private Practice', held in the Feelgoods' local, the Admiral Jellicoe, will long be remembered by those who were there – including our family tree artist Pete Frame (far right of top picture opposite).

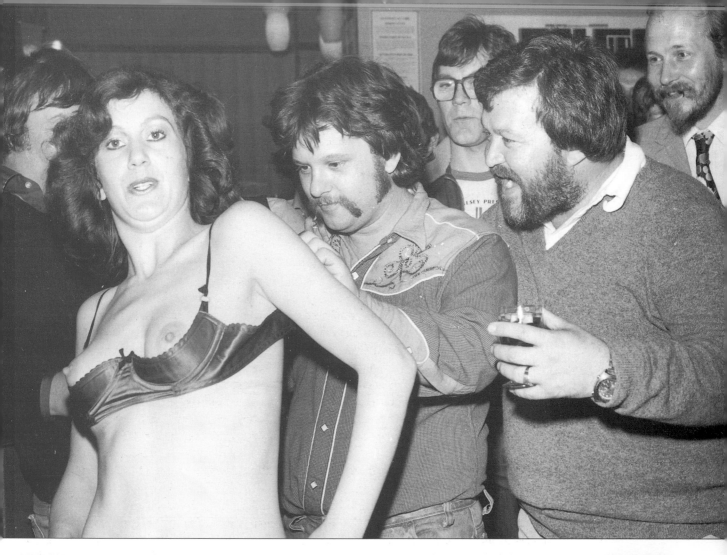

in Spain before coming home for a Christmas bash in England. Spain had always been something of a home from home for the band thanks to Chris's parents' holiday home in Almeria, Southern Spain, very near to the desert location at which several Spaghetti Westerns had been filmed. As Spain was then outside the EEC, it was illegal to take any substantial amount of Pesetas out of the country and all monies paid to the band for gigs had to be in US dollars. It was due to this technicality that Dr Feelgood found themselves involved in the fruit and veg export business...

The problem arose after the band had played three large halls for a well-known promoter. On the day that the band were due to return back to the UK, the promoter informed Chris, at the last possible minute, that he couldn't pay the band as agreed in US dollars. Instead Chris found himself back in his hotel room with a mountainous pile of money sitting on his bed – all of it in small-denomination Peseta bills. With no time to spare before their flight home Chris called the band into his room and explained the dilemma. The cash was coming with them.

Each member of the group set about stuffing as much money about their persons as was humanly possible. Later on at the airport everyone made it through the customs check...except Gypie who, with his Rod Stewart barnet and dark glasses, was vying for the role of 'most elegantly wasted rock star'. As such he would have probably got pulled anyway. However if there was any lingering doubt about it, the sight of a wad of loosely rolled-up notes sticking out his trouser pocket guaranteed it. They were rumbled.

Before long the whole band were assembled together in a back room surrounded by guards. As each member of the group ceremoniously placed his stash of notes on the table, so much wedge was being pulled out of various trouser fronts that an elderly official started waving his hands in the air in alarm and shouting 'No! No! No!' as each new wad hit the table.

Once again Chris Fenwick was the fall guy, quickly drawing the 'Go straight to jail card'. The band were permitted to depart for the UK while their hapless manager was detained (without his passport) over the whole Christmas period to answer serious charges of currency smuggling in the New Year. Eventually, after appearing in front of a local magistrate, he was allowed to proceed to the UK...only without the cash. Nearly nine months later he received a call which allowed him access to the loot. However it still hadn't clarified the ongoing problem of how to get money out.

The answer to this tricky problem was suggested by Chris's dad. Down in Almeria the White family and thus the Feelgoods had become friendly with a local fruit grower who routinely used to export his crop of melons and other sun-ripened produce to the UK. An improbable yet perfectly legal arrangement was soon cooked up whereby Dr Feelgood would pay him direct in Spain for his melons in Spanish Pesetas and his customer back in the UK would then pay Dr Feelgood the equivalent in Sterling. This continued annually until Spain joined the EEC and relaxed its regulations.

Having pursued a relentless touring schedule for the past year which hadn't allowed any time to think about or write material for a new LP, the band elected to keep things very simple and uncomplicated and to make their next one live. This would quickly deal with any record-company pressure and would also accurately reflect where they were at that point in time – which was out on the road.

The strategy known in Feelgood parlance as 'playing the live card' saw them team up once more with Vic Maile and put two shows down on tape, the resulting album 'As It Happens' slipping easily and undramatically into the racks in June 1979. It was, as ever, a typical cross-section of Feelgood material barked out to an appreciative audience. Unlike 'Stupidity', it wasn't going to change the world.

The record company were still very keen to have something newer from the band, perhaps with the odd hit single on it. Accordingly studio time was pencilled in among a very hectic touring schedule for later in the year. Once again, the pressure was on to deliver a whole album of new material – but first-choice producer Nick Lowe was unavailable. Through a connection with agent Nigel Kerr came the name of Mike Vernon, the man who'd produced Fleetwood Mac ('Albatross' and 'Man Of The World'), John Mayall and Focus.

As was by now standard practice, Mike went down to Canvey to routine the tracks prior to setting up in the studio – and once again there was something of a dearth of original material. Tracks such as 'Shotgun Blues' emerged from studio jams with Lee improvising a lyric, while others were pieced together in the studio. Vernon recalls himself and seasoned sessioneer Pete Wingfield, who'd been drafted in on piano, sitting in a back room hurriedly trying to write lyrics for backing tracks being recorded at the same time in the main studio.

Yet another producer was experiencing the Feelgoods' general dislike of the recording process. 'There was an element of the 99th hour,' Vernon diplomatically admits, adding that 'things weren't always earmarked as one would perhaps have liked them.' As Lee himself put it later on to Larry Wallis when discussing the whole recording

and writing dilemma, 'There aren't any Shakespeares in this group: we're not interested. We just want to play the fuckers, record them and get on.'

So it was that 'Let It Roll', the Feelgoods' sixth studio LP, was released in September replete with an amusing cover which reflected Lee's own growing antique collection by featuring each member of the band in the form of a foaming Toby jug. The album was generally well received, though it failed to deliver another hit in the mould of 'Milk And Alcohol'. The back sleeve, shot featuring a casual and relaxed-looking group sitting behind the bar at the infamous Cluedo Club in Feelgood House, supplied another glimpse of their way of life.

Larry Wallis recalls his times spent down on the Island, particularly one occasion when charismatic jazz singer George Melly was invited over for an after-gig drink. Melly, a larger than life showman in the Brilleaux mould, fitted well into the all-

drinking, all-smoking Cluedo crowd but had the ability to take things a notch further and 'camp things up'.

Wallis recalls the particular night in question when the Cluedo Club was in full alcoholic overdrive with Melly, as special guest, the centre of attention surrounded by some of the finest heterosexual specimens in Essex. It was at this moment that Warren Kennedy, brother of Feelgood road manager Dean and also a member of Eddie and the Hot Rods, made an appearance.

As Wallis recalls it, 'Melly's face instantly lit up, he grabbed him by the shoulders and said "What a beautiful boy!" and plonked a great big kiss on his cheek. There was this horrible frozen moment...and Chris Fenwick suddenly shouted out across the room "Don't 'it 'im!'" This is but one of many stories about the notorious Cluedo Club. The rest are currently locked away in a rock'n'roll vault under a 30-year rule, the names having been changed to protect the innocent.

A CASE OF THE SHAKES

By 1980, Dr Feelgood were, improbably to some yet none more so than themselves, celebrating an eighth successful year together. 'A Case Of The Shakes', their next studio recording, reunited them with producer Nick Lowe and was what Gypie affectionately refers to as 'a *real* Feelgood album'. After the usual rehearsal period the band went in to Eden Studios in London where they had previously recorded 'Private Practice'. This time, in order to ensure that they came up with the goods, they came mob-handed as far as songwriters were concerned, drafting in the talents of Larry Wallis and former Brinsley Schwarz keyboard player Bob Andrews, not to mention Lowe himself.

By that time, the producer recalls, 'they didn't mind breaking the mould a bit and trying something different. They were all getting on very well and from what I can remember, because again there was a lot of boozing going on, it was a better record than "Be Seeing You".' Confident and relaxed, the band settled in to record what was to emerge as a short, sharp, snappy collection of original pop songs.

Larry Wallis took to the task of writing for the Feelgoods with naked enthusiasm. 'I used to imagine Lee with that stabbing finger in my head. I'd pretend that I was him. It was a very strong image to write around, cut and dried, like you couldn't say "oh ah baby, the flowers are beautiful…" you had to say, "the cigar smoke was thick, and her legs were long." That worked fine.' Larry can also recall (vaguely, it has to be said) lying on his bed one night, under the influence of various mind-altering substances, with his guitar

effectively damaged his protégé whom he was grooming for pop stardom. 'I had him slimmed down looking like a proper rock star,' he complained, 'and the Feelgoods sent him back looking like a tub of butter.'

'A Case Of The Shakes' was yet another success, while the singles taken off it had picked up some useful airplay to keep the name of Dr Feelgood in people's minds. Meanwhile, the band continued to motor on relentlessly around the world. It was a pace that was bound, at some point, to start exacting a price.

Gypie Mayo, in particular, was starting beginning to feel increasingly dissatisfied with what he regarded as the general restrictions of

resting across on his chest – and coming up with the slightly spaced-out lyrics for what eventually became 'Going Some Place Else'.

The whole album was the most accessible and commercially 'poppy' the band had recorded, full of bright, punchy, sub-three-minute tunes very much in classic Nick Lowe mould. The LP sported a fun-looking graphic sleeve and garnered some very warm reviews. *Melody Maker* called it 'the best Feelgoods album ever and more…'

The only voice of dissent came from Jake Riviera, who was by this time Lowe's manager. He complained (with tongue very much in cheek) that the two-week stint spent in the studio had

R&B music – acutely aware in addition of the pressure to come up with new material every year. Back home in England he had a wife with a new-born son, while he found himself in far-away places like Australia and Japan, often more concerned about them than he was about the band. Little surprise, then, that he announced that he was taking himself off the road.

It wasn't only Gypie who was beginning to feel the pressure. Both Figure and Sparko had started to feel a similar urge to quit touring for a while and start to enjoy the fruits of their success. As Sparko recalls, the constant touring 'made you feel as if you were in the army, always being told where and

when to go somewhere.' Figure similarly likens it to being a 'biscuit salesman, forever out on the road selling.'

These rumblings were to continue among the band for the foreseeable future. The only person who seemed to thrive on this rigid environment was Lee, who apparently hadn't yet experienced every single culinary delight as suggested by his ever-handy Michelin guides. Brilleaux had married his longtime girlfriend Shirley in July 1981 and set up home in Leigh-on-Sea. However, a fully domesticated life was never on the cards. Home for any extended periods of time Lee would soon start to become restless: the road had become his way of life.

Will Birch: 'I think he carried a lot of what Americans call demons. I don't mean baggage, like he had hang-ups, but he was a very driven man. I always thought that something was eating him, he had something in him that made him want to tour, he had to get up on stage, that's what he did. He had it in his blood to entertain.'

Behind the scenes, record company-wise, things had changed as well. Andrew Lauder, the original A&R man who had signed the band, had left around the time of 'Be Seeing You' to establish his own record label, Radar. In the following years, the United Artists label was bought by EMI and, by the time 'A Case Of The Shakes' had been recorded, the Feelgoods found themselves as artists on a label where there was little interest in them. They had become like old bits of familiar furniture, to be shunted around at will.

Despite the fact they'd just recorded their best album in years, the band were beginning to slip in the marketplace. As Chris tells it 'We had traded down a lot by that time…we hadn't really delivered since "Milk And Alcohol", we'd had a few tries but we were in a diminishing market. These things happen. The relationship at EMI/Liberty was strained, and none of us were comfortable with the new situation.'

Rather than sit about crying over spilt milk and what might have been, Chris and the band elected once again to 'play the live card', deliver their last contractually-obliged record and get out. The delivery of this LP would also attract a substantial final payment which would at least secure the immediate future.

As a result, a mobile was booked and a show at Manchester University was laid down on tape and given the working title 'On The Job'. It was the last Dr Feelgood album for a major label – and also the last to feature Gypie Mayo whose guitar playing and personality had revitalised the band for so many years.

To ensure that the letter of their contract was observed and that they received their final payment from EMI without delay, Chris decided to deliver the master tapes for the album in person and to walk out with the final cheque safely locked in his briefcase. In managerial parlance this is called 'peace of mind'. After a bit of legal folderol, Fenwick walked out of EMI/Liberty as planned that afternoon with the 'substantial piece of action' safely in his possession.

He was now, for the first time in years, the manager of an unsigned band. Only this time, the future prospects were not so bright. The final payment for the live album would at least ensure that the band remained afloat in the coming uncertain months. However the relationship with EMI/Liberty was not, as was assumed, over quite yet – there were a few unexpected fun and games still to be had.

A short while later, Fenwick found himself inevitably out on the road with the band somewhere in Europe. He routinely called into the office to catch up with events and was informed that a very substantial cheque (just think of a number and shove a few noughts on the end) made payable to 'Dr Feelgood' had just arrived from, you guessed it, EMI/Liberty. Somewhere along the line, Liberty's arse had lost track of its elbow and another final contractual payment had been drawn up and put through the system. Dr Feelgood had effectively been paid off twice.

Seeing a real opportunity to create a bit of big-time mischief with some old sparring partners Fenwick decided to do nothing, sit on the cheque and wait for the inevitable fireworks. Bearing in mind that the sort of lolly we are talking about here is the kind of stuff that even hardened bank robbers get watery-eyed about, the very idea of all those straight-laced record company executives slowly realising the magnitude of their error was in

itself the source of great amusement. Chris was also keenly aware of the general perception that the Feelgoods were the sort of characters who would probably disappear with any extra loot that came through the post.

Chris was bemused to find that it was not until about about three months later that record-company shit started to hit the fan. During this period, Chris had sought additional advice from a cross-section of Canvey confidants. While some had advised he come clean (which was always his intention), other more colourful characters had suggested that he quit the country, put his feet up by the pool and let the record company do the singing for a change. Finally, the much anticipated panic call came in.

Fenwick retrieved the cheque from the bank and marched up to the record company to return their Monopoly money-sized kite. Ever keen to up the ante, he suggested that, since he'd travelled all the way up to London just to save a few accountants' bacon, it would be nice to take away a smaller cheque covering the modest recording costs of the last live LP, which Fenwick had originally decided to write off. He walked out of EMI for a second time with a much smaller, but nevertheless very handy, cheque in his pocket, a smile on his face and a story he still dines out on.

GOING SOME PLACE ELSE

lthough the band were no longer big hitters in terms of record sales, they were still earning a substantial amount as a touring act. Recalling the bitterness with which Heinz had recounted his various 'if only' stories to them years before, Dr Feelgood as a trading company had always invested substantial parts of their income into a whole cross-section of Canvey-based properties and small business units.

It may not have exactly have been hotel-trashing rock'n'roll, but it ensured that nobody associated with the 'firm' was going to end up at the age of 60 poncing about like some failed teenage pop star with little more than a couple of worn plectrums to rub together. Chris Fenwick: 'We wanted to make sure that we had something to show at the end of the gallop, because it will fall eventually – you can't keep jumping the fences forever. Eventually you will take a tumble and something is gong to catch you out.'

The Feelgoods, in short, were still in a strong position. The lack of a major record company to bankroll them was not in itself a big worry, and as a live draw they were still well able to dictate their own terms to promoters and club managers who were, as ever, always keen to pay less if they thought they could get away with it.

Once Gypie had decamped, the band once again set about the task of recruiting a new guitarist – a process Lee, in particular, didn't enjoy. It meant some basic moves had to be replayed: rehearsals, new publicity photos and a string of press interviews just to set the record straight. For a man who was really only interested in getting up on the stage, it was all an upheaval.

This time, despite being bombarded with all manner of weird and wonderful suggestions, the band elected to hold an open audition in order to recruit a new member. This was announced by a discreet advert in the back of *Melody Maker* which read 'Enthusiastic guitarist wanted for established R&B band'. This simple box ad was enough to flush out nearly every hip young gunslinger in the country, many of whom ended up at Feelgood House apprehensively tuning their guitars for a nervous run-through with the Doctors.

Among the odd assortment who turned up that day was a young guitarist called Gordon Russell

US-born Johnny Guitar (left) emerged from the ashes of the Chiswick label's Count Bishops to become the Feelgoods' third guitarist.

Road manager Dean Kennedy enjoys a rare spell in the spotlight on guitar.

who first showed each applicant the chords to the song that the band wanted to run through. One particular character Dean encountered seemed unsure of the best way to hold a guitar, let alone play it. Probing further, it transpired that he had seen a few people trooping into Feelgood House and had simply tagged along to see what was going on. Nice try.

Once inside, other over-enthusiastic characters, in a desperate bid to impress, slipped into highly acrobatic Wilko Johnson/Pete Townshend moves as they leapt and lurched around the studio flaunting their obvious rock-star potential. When asked afterwards to pose for a memory-jogging Polaroid, some would instantly reach for a glass of beer and hold it up gleefully just to ensure that their drinking credentials were recorded. Around the Feelgoods, it seemed everyone was going mad. Another prospective challenger who had managed to get through to the second round inadvertently crossed himself off the list by performing a turf-destroying handbrake turn on Chris Fenwick's immaculate croquet lawn as he triumphantly pulled away.

Gordon Russell recalls being quite nervous after plugging in his guitar for the first time. 'I thought I'd blown it on the first couple of numbers as I came in too early and they all said "just calm down".' It was then that Gordon discovered that Figure always counts the numbers in. After Gordon came Johnny Guitar, whose path had crossed the group's several times on the European gigging circuit while with the Count Bishops.

Johnny was also one of those called back, and when the decision came down to a choice between the two it was felt that Johnny had the edge. He was older, he had more experience plus the band vaguely 'knew' him. At the Admiral Jellicoe afterwards, he put away seven or eight pints which was yet another unconscious part of the recruiting process. The Feelgoods were active again.

Johnny describes the Feelgood camp which he suddenly found himself in as almost being like a 'gentlemen's club'. Lee had by this time developed an almost encyclopaedic and detailed knowledge of nearly every fine restaurant, cheese shop, butchers and bar in every town and city in Europe. Every day the band would delight in turning up at a particular restaurant and ordering (in fluent French, if appropriate) some of the finest food and wines available while still fully aware of the fact that they all looked like a pack of second-hand car dealers out on a day trip. This, then, was the established routine for the band which effectively made the daily grind of the touring process not only bearable but also highly enjoyable.

Johnny, however, had unwittingly walked into a volatile situation that was rapidly deteriorating.

and John Crippen, a more experienced hand with the stage name Johnny Guitar. Johnny recalls first seeing the ad which set his mind off racing as, in effect, there were only, two real 'name' R&B bands in the country – the Blues Band and the Feelgoods.

Chris Fenwick recalls that the day was to be a highly entertaining one. The first signs of this came early on in the morning when he had noticed a family saloon car parked discreetly in his driveway. Inside was a mum and dad accompanying a spotty-looking, guitar-toting son. They had all travelled down from some far-flung corner of Britain in the early hours of the morning 'just to make sure'.

Five hours, later with the band set up in the rehearsal room to the back of Feelgood House, the first candidates were being wheeled in. Before plugging in with the band each aspirant player was 'vetted' by Feelgood road manager Dean Kennedy

Both Sparko and Figure were still feeling increasingly unsettled by the relentless touring schedule. Sparko was slowly letting his daily alcoholic intake run his life. This was, after all, an environment where one could – and would – routinely order a Bloody Mary for breakfast in lieu of some freshly-squeezed orange juice and a bowl of cereal.

For the past ten years, the band had raised the art of drinking to something approaching a science. It seemed that virtually every picture taken of the band on every stage in Europe featured someone with a pint in one hand and a fag in the other. Boozing was always a 'Jolly Up'. On tour, various well-worn routes would be taken to ensure that particular pubs were regularly hit. At

hotels after gigs the band would, as a matter of course, hide away the steel rails that enabled the bar shutters to be hauled down. As a result, when Dr Feelgood were in town the bar literally couldn't close.

Sometimes, though, even this was no guarantee of lasting success. Tour manger Brian Pearson remembers vividly the night the band hit Limerick (during the Gypie days) and the after-gig bash that ensued... 'At about three o'clock in the morning the landlord said that's it.' Worried in case some offence had been caused, Brian probed more deeply. It was simple: the Feelgoods had drunk *all* the beer.

Johnny recalls Lee pulling a gag at the time which involved him dashing into a pub and shouting with some urgency 'Brandy! Quick! I'm a Doctor!' (a fact which was, after all, partly true). In response, a bottle and a glass would be produced and Lee would down the shot in one. In the tour bus, Lee was on one occasion ploughing through the pulp fiction novel *Beat The Devil*, which featured a lead character who would reply 'Busy Drinking' to any interruption to his routine. This quickly became both an established catchphrase and a standard reply to any enquiry.

After ten years on the road, however, the bottle was beginning to hit back. Sparko: 'The drinking thing was like a joke – no one could refuse a drink. It was like – excuse me? You don't want a drink? Can you write that down? No-one was allowed to refuse.' Partly as a result of this culture, by the time Johnny Guitar joined the group Sparko needed to come off the road and take a well-earned rest.

The Big Figure was also feeling the pressure. Leaving his family for months on end had always been traumatic, and with an annual gig count approaching the 300 mark he was never home with his wife and children who were growing up fast without him there to share it. 'It was like gig, gig, gig...home for a couple of weeks...pack bag, off again for another four weeks. It was a very busy time for us; we were away in the Far East, Japan and Australia and I really started to crack up a bit, I just felt I needed a break.'

Soon the internal pressures within the band started to reflect onstage as shows began to lose their distinctive sparkle and people began

to 'go through the motions' – the antithesis of what Dr Feelgood were all about. When Sparko decided to depart Figure felt that it would be an opportune moment for him to stand down too and give Lee a chance to replace the rhythm section wholesale.

With this scenario rapidly developing, the band had secured a one-off deal with Ted Carroll's Chiswick label to make another LP. Once again a familiar pattern emerged, as Johnny recalls: 'I'd just joined the band and it was time to make a record and all eyes looked to me...' Yet again, the band were casting about for enough suitable material to make an album. Johnny can remember hurriedly writing the lyrics to 'Crazy About Girls' on the train down from Fenchurch Street to Benfleet, the click-clack sound of the train's wheels on the rails acting as a metronome.

Other songs such as 'Rat Race' came with Johnny supplying a catchy lick and Lee improvising a lyric to fit. Squeeze tunesmiths Tillbrook and Difford were tapped for an original song called 'Monkey' and the whole album, which was entitled 'Fast Women And Slow Horses', was

recorded at Rickmansworth in June 1982, again with their old mate Vic Maile in the producer's chair. The LP was released to a generally lukewarm reception in the press.

With Sparko and Figure's subsequent departure, it was the end of an era which plunged both Lee and Chris into an uncertain and unsettled period. The band was crumbling…and yet had to remain a functioning touring unit in order to fulfil already confirmed commitments.

Figure had suggested the name of a possible replacement drummer – Buzz Barwell, a Southender who had previously played with both Wilko Johnson and Lew Lewis. Johnny Guitar pulled in his former Count Bishops mate Pat McMullen on bass, and the band hit the road to promote the new disc. Lee was reported in the press as saying about his new team, 'To be honest, if I close my eyes, I can hardly tell the difference. Sometimes I wish they'd relax a bit and go their own way…but they won't hear of it.'

It was a typical piece of Brilleaux grit in the face of adversity. For the reality was simple, as Gypie Mayo observes: 'Sparko plays a 12-bar walking

Perhaps the shortest-lived Feelgoods line-up included two ex-Bishops in Johnny Guitar (left) and Pat McMullen (right), with Buzz Barwell resplendent in biker jacket.

bassline by strumming it, the only bass player I know who does that. When you combine that with Figure's earthy drumming it sounds great – and that, for me, is the Feelgoods' sound.' The new line-up had effectively lost some of the vital chemistry which makes a good band great.

That summer, with a considerable amount of European work on the cards, the band rented a couple of villas in Spain to act as a convenient operational base. Chris Fenwick headed down to Spain to catch a few shows with the new outfit and he wasn't happy with what he saw. There was no getting away from it…the band, with the best will in the world, just wasn't as good as it should be.'

Johnny recalls that even the normally mild-mannered and ever-humorous Brilleaux was beginning to feel the pressure that all the changes had put on him. 'He was always great but, without Sparko and Figure, there was a different quality to it and he felt it. He always gave his all, but he became a little ratty towards the end. It wasn't fun any more.'

To Chris Fenwick, the name Dr Feelgood had always been a byword for just one thing – a blinding stage act. Now if that wasn't going to happen consistently then he felt the band was finished. With that in mind, Lee and Chris decided for the first time in ten years to pull the band off the road and take a break. It was 'make your mind up time'. Chris recalls that he had already decided to take the opportunity to go off for an extended six-week holiday in India; before he departed he spoke to Lee in strict managerial terms. 'When I come back, I want you to have a new line-up.'

I DON'T WORRY ABOUT A THING

11

While Chris wandered among the tea plantations of Central India, Lee set about rebuilding the band. One of the first people he contacted was Gordon Russell, the young guitarist who had impressed at the previous auditions. Gordon was regularly gigging around with Geno Washington and recalls that, when he spoke to Lee, it seemed the intention was to leave the name Dr Feelgood behind and go out as the Lee Brilleaux Band.

Gordon came down to Canvey, met up with Lee and had a jam session in a rehearsal room. It sounded encouraging. As the search to find other suitable musicians progressed, Lee would often go over to the Zero Six club at Southend Airport where every Monday night local musicians would turn up and jam with each other. A regular visitor to the club at the time was Phil Mitchell, the former schoolmate of Lee who, since that first stumbling juvenile gig, had stuck doggedly with

The Feelgoods' 1983 line-up was to last six years and featured with Lee, from left, Gordon Russell, Phil Mitchell and (foreground) Kevin Morris.

his bass-playing and was now a fully-fledged professional, having done stints with such local talents as Mickey Jupp and Lew Lewis.

Phil had already heard on the grapevine that Dr Feelgood had effectively spilt and so he approached Lee to find out what was on his mind. 'I said if you're thinking of getting a band together I'd love to be involved.'

Six weeks later, Chris returned wondering what he would find. It looked encouraging. A good gig offer had come in asking for Dr Feelgood to play a one-off in Monte Carlo. Lee contacted Gordon Russell and Phil Mitchell and asked them if they wanted to do the gig as a one-off to see how it went. With the Big Figure deputising, the quartet headed South.

The gig was to prove very successful. The band performed well to a very appreciative audience and the snap, crackle and pop had returned. It seemed Dr Feelgood still had legs. Chris Fenwick contacted agent Nigel Kerr, who started putting in a few more dates. Initially, Buzz Barwell filled in on

drums before finally departing, which was when Phil Mitchell suggested to Lee his old mate Kevin Morris.

Since his schooldays, Kevin had become a professional drummer who had cut his teeth on package tours in the early 1970s playing with the likes of Sam and Dave and Edwin Starr. He was currently occupying the stool in a French heavy-metal band called Trust – 'which wasn't really my scene.' It was, nevertheless, a regular paying gig. Upon getting the call from the more musically attractive Feelgood camp, however, he leapt at the opportunity and quickly came on board. He had a first rehearsal on a Monday and a gig at Dingwalls on the Wednesday.

By now, with a totally new line-up around him, Lee realised that it was make or break – the band were no longer the headline act they had once been and if they fell apart again it really could be over. To get back to the position they'd once occupied was going to necessitate serious graft. Accordingly, Lee rolled up his sleeves and climbed

back into the tour bus fully prepared to play at smaller venues, some of which the Feelgoods hadn't graced for many years. If they had to start again, at least everyone concerned was determined to make it work. Kevin: 'It was accepted that we were going to get it together, some we'll win and some we'll lose.'

Regrouped and refreshed, the band headed straight out on the road to reaffirm their reputation as *the* premier live English R&B band. Gordon Russell recalls that the pace was 'absolutely non-stop: five weeks in France, four weeks in Germany, two months in Scandinavia. It was unbelievable. I was forever sitting in that tour bus or on an airplane. It was the time of my life.'

Label-wise Dr Feelgood were still in something of a limbo. As no-one, it seemed, was going to offer them anything on a long-term basis. Chris and Lee elected to finance their next recording project themselves, they could then place it with the independent label of their choice. It was in this spirit that 'Doctor's Orders' was conceived with Mike Vernon re-engaged as producer.

Once again the band found themselves casting around for suitable material to record. Larry Wallis was drafted in to see if he had a few ideas and Mike Vernon was always ready to suggest a suitable cover. Gordon recalls that by the time the band went into record the LP they did have enough songs sorted out. 'I think we had pretty much prepared, because it was Feelgood money and Chris had seen previous LPs just pulling through so he was determined that we were only going into the studio when we were ready.'

Once there, though, the band still struggled to capture the live vibe which was their bread and butter. Mike Vernon suggested 'I Don't Worry About A Thing', which was laid down in one take. This was, as Kevin Morris agrees, 'very much the Feelgood style' whereas other tracks – such as 'Talk Of The Devil' – took much, much longer to record and were by comparison 'teeth pulling'. Kevin Morris was even to contribute some organ sounds to the track 'Drivin' Wheel', fixing strips of gaffer tape to the appropriate keys to help him hit the right notes. Despite these minor problems the band completed the sessions, which Phil Mitchell enthusiastically characterises as having been 'Big studio, big producer. Exciting!'

While the album was mixed, the band departed for Australia with rough 'off the desk' tapes they

were all very enthusiastic about. By the time they had returned to England, the LP was finished with the band left feeling that some of the rougher edges, which characterised their sound, had been smoothed over in the mix. Nevertheless, the band had a fine LP to promote, packaged in a suitably moody voodoo-like sleeve. This time it was the Jake Riviera/Andrew Lauder label Demon which picked the LP up in the UK with various one-off deals negotiated across Europe. Again the overall effect on the band was to raise their profile. The gigs were by now uniformly successful and the band were enjoying a new lease of life.

In the following year, 1985, the band started to discuss another set of recordings. Still without a natural writer in the band, the prospect of coming up with 12 new tracks seemed as daunting a process as ever. At the time, there was a fashion in the industry for the 'mini album', a 12-inch disc with five or six songs on it which U2 had pioneered with 'Under A Blood Red Sky'. Kevin Morris, picking up on this concept, suggested the idea of going into the studio and simply recording half a dozen of the band's favourite blues songs. Among them was one Gordon had suggested called 'Mad Man Blues', a John Lee Hooker track that Lee took to instantly.

The band went into Trackside Studios in Southend and, operating with just an engineer, laid down such classic cuts as 'Dust My Broom', 'My Babe', 'Tore Down' and 'Dimples'. This project was something of a return to the Wilko Johnson days of minimal overdubs and a live backing track. Listening to the results blasting out of the studio speakers, Lee declared 'That's the row we want people to hear...' The album was dubbed 'Mad Man Blues' and was issued originally on the ID label in France.

If the past few years had taught Chris anything about record labels, it was that when it came to Dr Feelgood only one person knew how to best handle the band – and that was him. Consequently, he and Lee decided to take a positive step and form their own record label, with the intention of releasing all future Dr Feelgood recordings as well as any they could license back from the original record labels. This would ensure that the back catalogue was still available, some albums from the UA days having already been deleted.

The label took the name Grand after Lee's favourite local hostelry the Grand Hotel, located just up the road from his house in Leigh-on-Sea. However, before Grand was in a position to release their first brand-new LP, Dr Feelgood found themselves briefly being courted by an old friend armed with bagfuls of other people's money...another adventure was soon under way.

HIT, GIT AND SPLIT

12

One day the phone rang down on Canvey. It was Dave 'Robbo' Robinson of Stiff Records fame, a man whom Chris Fenwick recalls with a broad grin as 'one of life's most charming characters – but after you hung up the phone after talking to him you checked your pockets to see if you still had your money there.'

By the time of the mid 1980s, Stiff – formed in 1976 by the charismatic duo of Jake Riviera and Dave Robinson – had, like the Feelgoods, fallen somewhat from the heights of success. Armed with such memorable slogans as 'when you kill time you murder success', Stiff had ended the 1970s the hippest record company in the country having nurtured such acts as Madness, Elvis Costello and Ian Dury.

But subsequent financial deals had sapped their strength and ten years later in 1986, Stiff was struggling to survive in a very competitive marketplace. Robinson was desperately trying to keep the name alive: he had regrouped the company, attracted some new finance and was once again ready to prove the self-proclaimed adage that 'If it ain't Stiff, it ain't worth a Fuck'.

Robinson invited Chris to come up to London to talk about some kind of record deal he had in mind

with the new-look Stiff. The idea behind this unexpected offer had, it transpired, come from another old friend of the band, Will Birch. 'I was doing quite a lot with Stiff, who were in terrible decline trying to stand alone as an independent. One day, myself and Dave were listening to an American R&B act and Dave asked me what did I think? I said if you're looking at that, then what about the Feelgoods? He said do you think they want to make a record? I said I'm damn sure they do.'

As Lee had been one of the original investors in Stiff, the whole notion felt oddly right to both Chris and Lee who had given up attracting the interest of a record label again. Despite the fact they'd recently established Grand, they figured that if someone else wanted to invest some money in the band it couldn't hurt. Chris negotiated a deal with Dave Robinson who, with a characteristic touch of blarney, signed Lee Brilleaux to Stiff with the words 'Lee's going to become my ambassador'.

It was, it seems, always Dave Robinson's plan from the outset to take the hard-boiled Feelgoods in a direction they had never really explored before. This was to be an overtly commercial marketing exercise, everything approached with a 'If that's what Dave wants, we'll give it a go' attitude.

Smart suits and slick haircuts were the order of the day as the Feelgoods signed to Stiff.

The scene in Southend's Trackside Studios, 1986, with producer Will Birch (left) and engineer Neill King (third from right) among the Feelgoods.

As a longtime friend of the band, as well as a record producer, Will Birch was very keen to combine the two roles. Additionally he had some of his own songs tucked away which he fully admits he was 'shamelessly trying to push forward.' Knowing the band as he did, Will was only too aware of the Feelgoods' general lack of interest in the more tedious aspects of the recording process coupled with their inherent weakness in the songwriting department.

It was motivated by these thoughts that, after first having convinced Dave Robinson that he was the man for the producer's job, he started collecting together a portfolio of songs to present to Lee. It was Will's feeling that if they were going to go in to record with Stiff they should try something of a new approach and not simply knock out a LP with '12 Chuck Berry tracks on it'. Will's selection was an eclectic mix which took in Johnny Cash's 'Get Rhythm' and even the Undertones' pushy-sounding 'You've Got My Number'. In addition, Larry Wallis had a song on offer, as did Gordon Russell, and the band were soon back in the studio working on an LP with the working title 'Southenders' – dreamt up by Dave as an ironic riposte to the popular BBC television soap opera *Eastenders*.

The sound Will was pursuing was a much softer, more organised and produced sound which was something of a departure. The band generally felt that it didn't really represent them as they were live. Some considerable time and effort was placed in the ballad 'Don't Wait Up', which had been written by Will Birch and Paul Astles and was clearly singles material. As Will recalls, 'it was a bit of a challenge for Lee to sing.'

The whole project was aimed at turning the rough and ready Feelgoods into something more like a R&B-tinged pop band, a process that involved a lot of production effort. Generally, Will found that the band responded, as ever, more successfully to a more direct and spontaneous approach in order to capture their powerful live sound. With Lee's voice 'the key was to catch a performance – so what you did was hit "record" when he was peaking, take a couple of good ones and then edit them together. He wasn't the sort of guy to whom you'd say – can you do that particular line again? He wouldn't be interested.'

The resulting LP was recorded in seven days. On hearing 'Don't Wait Up' Dave Robinson asked for a remix, at which point Will added a harmony voice behind Lee's to try an achieve a smoother, more radio-friendly sound. The track eventually appeared as a single which picked up much radio play. It wasn't exactly the familiar smokin'n'boozin' Feelgood sound – but, as Birch remarks, 'it was the first time I had heard Dr Feelgood on Radio One for quite a few years.'

Despite this success, the overall approach was one that the band as a whole were increasingly uncomfortable with. The LP title had suddenly changed overnight and was now known simply as 'Brilleaux', the cover of which featured Lee involved in a very 'Stiff-looking' piece of artwork. Again it had been Dave's idea to get a shot of Lee posing with a harmonica wedged sideways in his mouth. Although not a typical Brilleaux image, it was very striking and soon featured on huge posters which Stiff had, it seemed, plastered on every wall and corrugated fence in London.

Though it appeared a solo career had been launched, with the rest of the band relegated to the role of session musicians, there was no doubt that all of this was conspiring to raise the profile of the band. On the gigging front, Dr Feelgood were, for the first time in quite a few years, selling out larger venues such as the Town and Country Club in Kentish Town and the Cambridge Corn Exchange. They may not have sounded like themselves on record, but there could be no doubt about who the outfit was on the live front.

Still looking for that elusive hit record which would really do it for both Stiff and the band, the next project Dave Robinson had in mind was a one-off single of a version of the rock'n'roll standard 'See You Later Alligator'. On this occasion, the band didn't even perform the main backing track. They'd returned from tour to be presented with Dave Edmunds in the studio and a fully sequenced track ready and waiting for a vocal and some guitar to be laid down on top of it.

It was so well organised that Gordon Russell felt that even Dave Edmunds wasn't sure why he was there beyond lending his name as producer to the project. The resulting track was again a radical departure from the Feelgood sound but nevertheless something which was to become a surprise hit record for the band in Sweden – a fact soon translated into two months of live work.

Still determined to break the Feelgoods into a bigger market, Dave Robinson had a few more ideas up his sleeve – but before he could instigate them Stiff hit the buffers again. Chris Fenwick recalls hearing whispers about Stiff on the grapevine: 'The next thing I know there's a creditors' meeting announced. Stiff owe over a million and a half pounds and I just think "fucking hell".'

Fenwick subsequently went along uninvited to the meeting in an attempt to find out where he and the band stood. Was there a record company any more or not? Chris: 'What transpires is that there is a "hive down". No-one is getting paid and all contracts are being handed over as an asset to another company.' The knight in shining armour riding in to save the legendary Stiff name was Jill Sinclair of ZTT Records, the label that made its fortune with Frankie Goes To Hollywood.

Suddenly Dr Feelgood, along with all the other various Stiff acts, was simply another asset to be handed around the boardroom without any say in the matter. Chris: 'It's taking the piss. If you pulled that sort of thing down here on Canvey you'd get your house burned down.' Despite this criticism, Fenwick realised that at least he wasn't actually owed anything: Jill Sinclair was willing to revive the ailing Stiff with an injection of much-needed cash and the show could go on. Captain Dave Robinson was still on board and once again keen to convert the Feelgoods into a multi-million selling act.

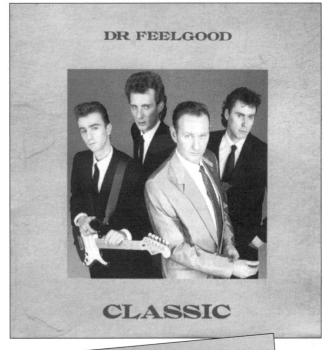

This time his strategy to achieve this was more direct – throw some money at the project and make it happen. As a result, he hired the successful producer Pip Williams, who had recently had a big hit with Status Quo. Producers like Williams, partly because of the massive sales they can sometimes engender, don't come cheap. Nor do the studios they like to work in. As a result the next LP was to cost Stiff the sort of money that Dr Feelgood could have quite happily cut five or six more down-to-earth records out of and still have had change for a few rounds down at the Jellicoe. Still, it wasn't their shout.

If the previous record, 'Brilleaux', had been 'produced', what was to eventually be called 'Classic' was Hollywood with brass knobs on. The band again pieced together a selection of originals including some from Will Birch and Kevin Morris along with some improbable covers such as Dylan's 'Highway 61'. The resulting album was predictably a very polished, very 1980s record, which with the addition of various horns, keyboards and backing singers further buried the Feelgoods under layers of production. As Gordon Russell says: 'It just wasn't like we sounded.'

Kevin Morris can recall the recording process as being 'very clinical and, for us, very hard work. Lee found it very difficult.' And yet, as Phil

Mitchell remarks, 'Lee was a very professional man. He did what was asked of him and he didn't feel bad about doing it, although I sometimes think he felt uncomfortable.'

Confirmation of the makeover which the band was undergoing came in the cover of the resulting record which featured the Feelgoods decked out in the manner of an American 1950s outfit complete with greased-back quiffs and sharp-looking shiny suits. The pictures were taken by a very well-regarded photographer called Simon Fowler more at home with real pop stars like Simply Red. Through his lens, the Feelgoods emerged looking like a waxwork pop group.

Soon after the record was eventually released, Jill Sinclair and Dave Robinson almost inevitably fell out – and, as Chris put it, 'we're back out on the streets.' From this moment on, he elected to stick to his original plan and stay firmly rooted on Canvey, releasing everything past, present and future on Grand Records. The two Stiff LPs were, in fact, among the first to be rescued from obscurity and reissued.

Stiff, *the* label of the late 1970s and early 1980s, was suddenly history and an experiment in marketing in which the Feelgoods had featured as guinea pigs was finally over. Normal service was soon resumed.

THE FEELGOOD FACTOR

13

Whatever the reservations about the the Stiff interlude, it had done the band no harm at all as a live draw. In much the same way that the arrival of Gypie Mayo had revived the band's fortunes after Wilko, the new post-Sparko/Figure band with Gordon Russell saw them gradually re-establish itself on stages across Europe as a premier R&B outfit. With the shows uniformly firing on all four cylinders, it seemed that nothing could stop the band. Nothing that is…except the unexpected.

While returning from a four-week jaunt to New Zealand, Gordon Russell was informed that his recently-born child had tragically died of cot death syndrome. At about the same time, Lee Brilleaux had similarly received the news that his father had passed away. Gordon was totally distraught and simply in no position to climb back into the tour bus. Lee, on the other hand, responded to his own

bad news by characteristically seeking the road as something of a comfort, perhaps a more familiar place to forget things than even home.

With confirmed dates already set up in Greece, the band fulfilled these obligations by pulling in Gypie Mayo on guitar. Gordon, meanwhile, took a few weeks off in France where his girlfriend at the time lived. It was during this sojourn that he decided to leave the Feelgoods in order to come off the road which he had been constantly travelling for nearly five years. As a final gesture, Gordon agreed to one last tour before reluctantly parting company with the band.

Yet again the Feelgoods found themselves desperately seeking a new guitarist. On this occasion there was a name of someone already featuring in the band's conversations – Steve Walwyn. Steve was a versatile and very accomplished guitarist whom the band had first come across in previous years when he had played with Midlands-based band the DTs who had supported the Feelgoods on several occasions. Later Steve had worked with ex-Small Face Steve Marriott, who had also supported the band at the Town and Country Club. As Kevin puts it, 'We always liked his guitar playing and had thought secretly that if Gordon ever did leave we'd give him a shot.'

Steve was quickly tracked down and phoned up (somewhat embarrassingly for him, while doing a soundcheck for another group). He quickly agreed to come down to Canvey to have a try-out with the band. With this in mind, Kevin sent him up a list of proposed songs and Steve turned up at Dave Higgs's rehearsal rooms on Canvey. (The legendary Feelgood House had by this time been vacated as Chris Fenwick had moved off the island to join the rest of the world on the mainland.)

Steve can recall setting his gear up while Lee immediately put him at his ease by saying 'Don't worry too much about the arrangements, we just want to see if you've got the spirit right.' Half-way

through the run through, Lee discreetly glanced over to Kevin and gave a thumbs-up sign. When everyone repaired to the Lobster Smack to test the counter, Steve hit the bar first, asking everyone what they wanted. Lee drily said to Kevin, 'Well, he's passed the pub test.' The band had their man.

Steve was eased in with a few gigs around the country before the Feelgoods took a two-week break. After that they returned to play at the Town and Country in London. At the best of times, this would be a high-profile, 'pressure' gig – and on this occasion it would be prove to be doubly so when it transpired that proceedings were being filmed for a television special. It was to prove one of the few occasions when anyone in the band had actually seen Lee displaying nerves in response to the fact that they had barely broken in Steve.

On the night the new boy acquitted himself well: there may have been the occasional wrong chord, but overall it had all the hallmarks of a Feelgood gig – power and excitement. Afterwards the band were offered the chance to purchase the

Steve Walwyn (third from right) slotted into the place vacated by Gordon Russell.

multi-track tapes from the mobile which had recorded the television sound. Listening back to them, they were impressed with the overall quality and vibe of the performance and quickly decided to put them out on Grand as the LP 'Live In London'. As Kevin puts it: 'Any line-up change is a jolt: it inevitably kicks everything up the arse and you naturally look at the set and put in some new songs, change the arrangements. It's a new impetus. Steve lifted us up.' This LP proves it.

Once again – as was the case with Gypie, Johnny and Gordon before him – Steve plugged straight into a full calendar of live dates as the band returned to prowl the road. By this time, the relentless 250-date a year schedule had started to be deliberately pruned down. Even someone like

Lee, who lived and breathed the road, appreciated the need to take the pace down a few notches and spend a little more time at home with his wife, Shirley, and their two young children.

It was on these occasions that Lee would slip into something of a 'off-road' routine by frequenting the familiar surroundings of his local pubs – the Crooked Billet and the Grand Hotel in Leigh-on-Sea, often arriving via the bookies. At the Grand, Brilleaux would have his own familiar perch at the end of the bar and if he wasn't diligently working his way through his *Daily Telegraph* crossword, he would be mixing it more vociferously with the equally charismatic characters who also inhabited the saloon bar. These included Dickey Boy, Colin the Socialist and

Graham the Shed, not to mention Dennis the Dog and Ron the Kite – all people who, as Chris Fenwick puts it, 'make me look like a choirboy.'

Lee had developed something of an off-stage persona which slotted well into the odd bohemia of the Grand. Larry Wallis refers to it as being a cross between something out of PG Wodehouse and Damon Runyon. Brilleaux was also something of a raconteur who could also turn his hand to the odd impression in order to make a witty point, often mixed with some 'off the wall' surrealism. Figure recalls Lee bringing to life such memorable characters as 'A Broken Bottle' or 'An Elephant in the Bar' and even 'Larry the self-wanking Penis' to amuse those around him. He had, as Chris puts it, 'a satirical mind.'

Business-wise, back on Canvey, Chris had employed a familiar face, Will Birch, to temporarily assist him with the everyday administration of Grand Records. Will was as keen as ever to get back into the studio again with the Feelgoods. He suggested the idea to Chris, and the next LP project was soon under way. Titled 'Primo', Birch approached it in much the same way as he had previously at Stiff by putting together a compilation of suitable material for the band to consider. Once again, this comprised some original songs penned by himself along with other cover choices very much in keeping with the Feelgood ethic.

There was, for example, a Mickey Jupp song 'Standing At The Crossroads Again' along with 'Heart Of The City' by old mucker Nick Lowe (Stiff's first ever single) and 'World In A Jug' by Canned Heat. Other choices such as the Doors' 'Been Down So Long' seemed somewhat esoteric to say the least. It was as Kevin was to put it 'The usual mish-mash of material.' However, the sessions did provide the band with several great tracks like 'Down By The Jetty (Blues)' and 'If My Baby Quits Me', which were soon to become

established parts of the ever-developing stage show.

With Will's pop sensibilities still to the fore, the band recorded four tracks at the Greenhouse in London. It was midway through this period that Phil Mitchell decided to leave the ranks, having become the latest victim of the Feelgoods' perennial disease...road fatigue. Phil had been struggling for some time to juggle various domestic problems with the life of a touring musician. He had begun to take his foot off the accelerator and coast. By mutual agreement he stepped down.

To carry on with the immediate recording sessions the band recruited Inmates bass player Ben Donnelly before finally settling on a full-time replacement for Phil. This turned out to be Dave Bronze, a well regarded session player who lived just round the corner from Lee, Kevin and Chris in Leigh-on-Sea. Dave was initially hired to complete

'Primo', eventually released on Grand in June 1991. As far as Dave was concerned, these sessions were as far as his role in the band was due to go. The band, however, had other ideas.

Dave had worked well with everyone, and so a short while later Lee contacted him and asked if he'd be up for a one-off date in France. Dave agreed. The preparations for it were, as Dave recalls, typically Feelgood. 'I got an afternoon rehearsal for two hours and then we got in the van and headed to France.'

After this, a few more dates were on the cards and again Dave was invited to do them. 'At the time I was thinking of them as a one-offs and then more gigs came along. There was never really any conscious moment when I joined the band.' Conscious or not, Dave gave the band a new injection of enthusiasm which resulted in Lee stating at one point that it was the best Feelgood line-up ever.

As Chris Fenwick recalls, 'It really cracked along. There was a real edge to it live.' To make the point, Chris can recall the band playing a live GLR radio session at which the DJ was located upstairs in a different studio from the musicians down in the basement.

After introducing the band, they launched smartly straight into a number which was whipped to an end in under three minutes. The attack was so decisive that, in the moment's silence after the track ended, the DJ was caught 'on air' unawares asking incredulously 'was that live?'

Similarly, Will Birch recalls a gig the band played at the Town and Country Club which saw Lee, dressed in an immaculate powder-blue suit, taking control of the audience while the band kicked into gear behind him. 'They opened with "King For A Day". Lee walks up to the mic and he's towering over the audience (who by this time are already going wild). The charisma and showmanship was massive, the lights were right, the band were right and the way he snatched that microphone it was really exciting. He could read a room.' As Dave Bronze was to put it more succinctly: 'Lee never took prisoners!'

The band were on tip-top form, gigging when they liked and releasing records on their own label. They had attained the position that most recording artists simply never see in their creative lifetimes – artistic control. Once again, it seemed, that the only thing that could stop the Feelgoods from rolling on for ever was the unexpected.

KEEP IT OUT OF SIGHT

14

Chris Fenwick has an amusing image he sometimes employs to describe the inherent problems of working with a band, any band. His theory is that packed away in every band's flightcases there is such a thing as the 'troublemaker flag'. Under normal circumstances the flag lies dormant on the floor and it is the manager's job to make sure that it stays there. Occasionally someone, for whatever reason, will pick it up and perhaps flutter it at knee level before quickly putting it down again, having made their particular point.

On other, more serious, occasions, the 'troublemaker flag' is picked up, waved furiously above head height and the message is clear.

Chris: 'This is the point when, if they don't put it down, the person waving it generally speaking has to leave.' As a description of the internal mechanics of a band it's a great metaphor. Inevitably in a management career spanning some 20 years Fenwick has seen the 'troublemaker flag' waved high and low on numerous occasions.

One day, as Chris recalls, Lee came into the office to have a chat. It was to be a meeting he would never forget because, for the first time ever, it was Lee who was waving the 'troublemaker flag'. Chris was taken aback: 'I thought you're the guv'nor, what are you starting for?' Something was definitely up.

Around the time of 'Primo's recording, those around Lee like Kevin Morris and Will Birch had begun to notice that he was generally not himself health-wise. As Will recalls, 'If there was a cold in the air he would have it.' From the moment he joined the band, Dave Bronze also felt that perhaps Lee was somehow not the full monte. Uncharacteristcally, Lee had started to become short-tempered over silly, trivial matters when things weren't exactly slotting into place. It was a character trait no-one had ever experienced before.

Chris was so concerned about Lee's perceived mood at the time that at the end of the season, with Lee sitting in the office, he put it to him directly.

'Reluctant' recruit Dave Bronze (right) added both songwriting and production skills to the Feelgoods' ranks on his arrival in 1991.

'Do you want to do this any more? Because if you don't, don't just do it for me, because you seem to be a bit pissed off with it all...' Lee's reply was: 'I like it more than I don't...'

Unbeknown to everyone at the time, including himself, Lee was displaying the first symptoms of the illness which was to finally claim his life. This manifested itself physically in the form of a small lump on his neck which he subsequently attended a hospital to have it removed and tested. Towards the end of the year, it was clear that he was unwell. Dave Bronze recalls Lee coming offstage after a high-octane gig with a temperature of a hundred. As this situation gradually unfolded, Chris contacted agent Nigel Kerr and gigs which had been pencilled in for the coming months were discreetly stood down while the situation was further investigated.

With the actual band in tip-top condition and playing some of the best music they had ever played, a new recording project was soon being eagerly discussed. The first discussions took place while the band were out on the road, as Lee himself so eloquently put it on the later sleevenotes to the resulting LP 'The Feelgood Factor' – 'on a ferry plying between mainland Scotland and the Orkney Islands sometime in Autumn '92. I seem to recall being relatively sober but cruelly tormented by a vicious hangover. The latter was significantly alleviated by a judicious intake of the barley waters prevalent in those parts, but more particularly by the collective enthusiasm for the project in hand; it's not often that the muse and mammon sit well together.'

For the first time since the Wilko Johnson era, the band had within its ranks a definite songwriting capability in the shape of Steve Walwyn and Dave Bronze, with Kevin also capable

of penning a song or two. There was a real confidence alive in the band with everyone determined to go into the studio with fully worked-out and lyrically sound songs, thereby side-stepping the traditional Feelgood ritual of 'knock it up and see' in the studio process.

Steve and Dave accordingly set about writing a selection of songs for the proposed LP. The band then rehearsed for the coming sessions above the Grand Hotel before decamping to Monnow Valley Studios in Wales. Originally the band intended to use their old stomping ground at Rockfield, where they'd first recorded 'Down By The Jetty' almost 20 years before, but it had by this time upgraded its equipment and become something of an up-market country retreat. The old desk and other equipment, however, had been installed at another smaller, associated studio just a short drive away at

the Old Mill House – effectively Rockfield in another guise.

In late February, the band booked the studio, loaded the van up with equipment and enough food and wine to keep them going for the duration and headed for the Welsh border. Dave Bronze was both playing bass and co-producing with Dave Charles from Monnow. The routine at the studio was relaxed and confident, as Kevin recalls: 'If I wasn't drumming I'd cook; if Lee wasn't singing he'd cook: it was a very steady relaxed pace.'

With many strong songs on board, the session was conceived as a 'back to basics' project in reaction to the previous few LPs which had virtually emasculated the band. As Lee later explained on the sleevenotes, 'It was agreed that the songs would be straightforward and that they would be recorded straightforwardly and that they

Dave Charles, formerly drummer with United Artists labelmates Help Yourself, co-produced 'The Feelgood Factor'.

would be played and sung by members of Dr Feelgood without the unnecessary augmentation of a plethora of session musicians, backing singers and guest appearances…' Despite the fact that Lee was visibly feeling poorly, he paced himself for the duration and performed to his usual high standard. It was the most confident and aggressive album the band had recorded in some years, and everyone seemed to know it.

Midway though these sessions, Lee was called away to attend the hospital in London where he received the news that was to confirm the seriousness of his rapidly-deteriorating health. He was diagnosed formally as having lymphoma – a cancer which attacks and spreads throughout the lymphatic system. Back in Wales, the band remained oblivious and pressed on with the job in hand – overdubbing guitars and generally preparing other tracks ready for Lee to record his vocals upon his return. In his absence, Kevin Morris laid down a guide vocal on 'Lying About Blues', just to keep the ball rolling.

As a result of this enthusiastic pace, by the time Lee returned to Wales he was confronted with half a dozen tracks which all needed his voice. At this point Lee made no mention of the devastating news he'd been given, choosing instead to press on with the project in hand.

Dave Bronze recalls that on the day he returned 'I put him straight into the studio and basically roasted him. We must have done six or seven vocals, which is a lot for anyone to do.' Lee performed with his usual mic-shattering defiance and the sessions were soon completed.

At the end of the day, with his parts done, he revealed to the band the full extent of his illness and the fact that he had to go into hospital immediately to undergo a course of chemotherapy. Everyone was shocked by the news, which was tempered with a strange euphoria as the sessions had gone so well. Lee had completed what was to be his last studio recordings in the form of the punchiest and most confident LP Dr Feelgood had recorded in years.

As Lee headed back to London for medical treatment, Chris Fenwick pulled out the last booked dates from the date sheet, laid off the band and effectively put Dr Feelgood in mothballs. Whatever happened next was going to be anyone's guess.

DOWN BY THE JETTY (BLUES)

15

During the rest of March '93 at Feelgood HQ on Canvey, Chris pondered the rest of year ahead with apprehension. This was one 'troublemaker flag' that even he couldn't make disappear. The band was in limbo and his best friend was seriously ill. After Wales, the other members of the band had dispersed and established themselves in other bands. Steve Walwyn tied up with the Big Town Playboys, Dave Bronze with the Hamsters and later on as a member of Eric Clapton's touring band and Kevin Morris with Sid Griffin and Mick Taylor.

The chemotherapy process that Lee had to endure during the year of 1993 was, as most cancer sufferers will attest, almost worse than the illness it is seeking to combat. Because of the specific nature of his illness and the susceptibility to outside infection, he was contained for the duration within a 'reverse barrier' whereby all visitors have to gown up and enter a totally hermetically-sealed environment. Even though the original prognosis was not good, everyone knew that Lee Brilleaux was a fighter.

As is often the case in adversity, situations suddenly evolve from which strength can be taken. On this occasion it was to come from a very unexpected and somewhat nostalgic source. Chris Fenwick's brother Brian, 'Chalkie' to his friends, had followed his father's footsteps into the building and construction business. As a successful builder and property developer, he'd been responsible for many of the bright new house developments which had sprung up across Canvey in the 1980s.

Chalkie had recently acquired a development site on the Island which had a dilapidated old property standing on it. It was his intention to tear down the old and rebuild a smart new hotel on the site. The property was the Oyster Fleet, the somewhat run-down drinking house in which the original South Side Jug Band had cut their teeth.

Knowing that the Feelgoods were for the time being off the road, Chalkie made his brother Whitey an offer he couldn't refuse. This was to assume the role of manager and take on the old Oyster Fleet as a going concern for the time being. As his brother put it, 'Do what you like with it but when I say get out, get out.'

The old boozer still had a valid license and so Chris, along with Feelgood road manager Dean Kennedy and his wife Kim, set about transforming the run-down pub into the Dr Feelgood Music Bar. After years spent walking into all manner of weird and wonderful clubs all around the world, Chris and Dean now found themselves on the other side of the bar: the poachers had become the gamekeepers.

One of the team employed to help transform the old boozer into a proper music venue was Sparko. 'I was involved in the building of it, changing it from a scruffy old pub into an even scruffier club.' With a stage and an in-house PA system soon rigged, the doors were opened for business in early September '93 and bands were soon being booked in.

Remarkably, the bar seemed to take off very quickly with everyone concerned feeling that it already possessed something of an atmosphere of its own which seemed to guarantee a good night, whoever was up on the stage. Attracted by the name Dr Feelgood, fans of the band from outside the immediate area started turning up to discover the place for themselves and watch the likes of the Inmates, the Hamsters, Nine Below Zero and Canned Heat belting out their rough-hewn blues.

On other evenings, there was an open-door policy in operation and musicians' workshops evolved whereby all manner of local musicians would drop in for impromptu jam sessions. Dave Bronze and Gypie Mayo cropped up in the reggae favourites Elvis Da Costa and his Impostors, while the Big Figure appeared, again with Gypie, in the Shadows cover outfit the Six O'clock Shadows. Both Figure and Sparko were to become very regular fixtures in the bar, regarding it as simply 'our kind of place'.

The project had effectively provided everyone involved in the Feelgood camp with something to throw their prodigious energies into and also to take their minds off the slowly-evolving day-to-day situation with Lee. By the time the bar had opened, Lee had completed his painful course of chemotherapy. Larry Wallis was among the many friends who had dropped in to see Lee while he was still in hospital in London. 'He called me and said he needed a big cream cake, a newspaper and, more importantly, a single malt. I said to him are you going to be all right? He said "The jury's still out on that old boy, don't quite know yet."'

Shortly afterwards Lee was out of hospital and back down at his home, (wittily dubbed the

Down at the other Doctors. Chris Fenwick and proprietor David White (no relation) in a German version of the Feelgood Bar.

40 LEIGH TIMES GROUP November 9, 1993

DR FEELGOOD OPEN MUSIC BAR

ESSEX rhythm 'n' blues band Dr Feelgood, have now opened their own pub in Knightswick Road, Canvey.

Dr Feelgood, currently off the road to allow singer Lee Brilleaux to recover from a recent illness, are diverting their energies into the old Oyster Fleet, Canvey Island, now re-christened, "Dr Feelgood's Music Bar".

Reminiscent of the hostelries where Dr Feelgood cut their teeth in the early seventies, the pub offers the very finest real ales, plus live music four nights a week, including a weekly Monday blues jam.

Attractions

Recent attractions have included local favourites, The Abdabs, veteran rockers The Inmates and Dr and the Medics, with future attractions including the very best acts from Essex, London and further afield.

DR.FEELGOOD MUSIC BAR

21 KNIGHTSWICK ROAD, CANVEY ISLAND, ESSEX

TEL: 0268 682318

FEBRUARY

TUES 1 QUIZ NIGHT

WED 2 R+B BAND MIDNIGHT SPECIAL ADD £1-00

THUR 3 BEST-IN SKA · REGGAE · BLUEBEAT REGGAE SOUNDS

FRI 4 BACK TO THE 60'S ACID DAZE DISCO

SAT 5 LIVE BLUE'S BAND ADD £1-00 CHICAGO SHOUTHOUSE

TUES 15 QUIZ NIGHT

WED 16 LIVE R+B £1-00 OFF THE RAILS

THUR 17 007 SOUNDS ROCK STEADY FROM BASEMENT RECORDS PLAY AND SELLING THE BEST IN

FRI 18 TAKE A TRIP ACID DAZE PLUS LIVE MUSIC WITH FRIDAY I'LE PLAYED

SAT 19 FROM THE U S A £2 00 BLUE'S WITH LITTLE JIMMY KING

Proceeds) in Leigh-on-Sea. It seemed for a while that his illness was in remission and he started to put on a little much-needed weight (hence the cream cakes) and was once again being spotted in the Crooked Billet and the Grand having a few pints with his cronies. Lee also became a regular at the Feelgood Music Bar, where he would often give an encouraging word to some aspirant band or performer.

It was here that Sparko remembers having several nostalgic conversations with Lee when they had mused on the odd way that everything in their lives seemed to have come full circle. Once, as kids, they had both busked outside and inside the place in which they were now sitting which bore the name of the band that Sparko had dreamt up. Lee even floated the the idea of getting the Jug Band back together to play a one-off in the bar.

While Lee was in no position to front Dr Feelgood, he kept himself busy. In September, he and Shirley took their two children off on a trip to Disneyland. He also wrote the odd article for *Mojo* magazine and did the occasional radio interview, among them one with Paul Jones where Lee spoke with memorable understatement about his current health problems. As ever, he sounded full of optimism for the future – and, like the good pro he was, ensured the Feelgood Music Bar was heavily plugged.

However the optimism was to be short-lived, and towards the end of the year it seemed that the illness was once again active in Lee's system. Further chemotherapy seemed inevitable and, by Christmas he was clearly still a very unwell man. He nevertheless donned his best velvet smoking jacket and appropriate Christmas hat and ensured his children and those of Chris Fenwick had 'the best Christmas yet.'

It was during this festive period that Lee pulled Chris to one side and told him that he wanted him to arrange a couple of Dr Feelgood gigs at the music bar and record them. Fenwick greeted the idea with caution. Lee was still very poorly and the band hadn't played together for nearly a year. He suggested that perhaps he maybe should wait a more few months until his strength had built up: 'You might feel a bit better…' 'Yeah and I might feel a bit worse' was the hard-baked reply.

In the new year Chris started to organise the proposed event, still with a great deal of apprehension. 'He was very ill. I thought I don't want it to look bad, it'll make him feel worse: should I put a block on it and shut it down?'

Dave Bronze was contacted, not only as a band member but as producer for the proposed recordings. Dave recalls also being somewhat taken aback at the idea – but then Lee Brilleaux wasn't the sort of man you said no to. Dave wanted

to record the event with a small mobile set-up. 'The brief I set myself was that whoever was listening to it must feel that they are there. It has to be like you can smell the smoke and the beer is sticking to the floor. It had to be like that.' Dave, in effect, became musical director.

In January the band assembled and set about a series of rehearsals during the day in the Feelgood Bar. During these run-throughs, the by-now quite frail Brilleaux would sit up on the stage and work out with the band. Everyone was by this time very concerned as to Lee's ability to perform. But he soldiered on and by the end of January was ready to get up in front of a live audience and once again front the band that was his life. A picture taken around the time for the cover of the LP features a mischievous as ever Lee in trademark sheepskin lighting up a fag in a reprise of the 'Sneakin' Suspicion' cover.

On the night of the gigs, the bar was inevitably packed to the gills with people who wanted to see the band and Lee play together again. To ensure everything ran smoothly, Chris had arranged for two guest singers – Barrie Masters from Eddie and the Hot Rods and Bill Hurley from the Inmates – to front the band from the outset on each of the two evenings. This would take some of the pressure off Lee, who could then take the stage at his own pace and perform his set, knowing that if for any reason he wasn't up to it he could hand the mic over and the show would go on.

An additional worry was security. Lee wasn't as robust as he could be and there would inevitably be a lot of people who naturally wanted to get close to him. Over the two nights, Chris employed 'Cousin Gary' to act as Lee's minder, with the brief to get him safely on and off the stage and also to ensure that he had a bit of room around him to breathe. Once again, his old mate was backing him up just as he had all those years ago when they had wandered into Chinatown together. 'I told Gary to stand by his side and if anyone starts coming on get rid of them, don't wear gloves, be quick because I don't want him cornered. I was trying to protect him.'

So it was that, on the nights of 24 and 25 January 1994, Lee Brilleaux and Dr Feelgood played what was to be their last engagement together. To supplement the sound, Dave Bronze had augmented the basic line-up of Steve Walwyn, Kevin Morris and himself with sometime Kink Ian Gibbons on keyboards. With Lee perched on a high bar stool and dressed immaculately as ever, he soon took control of the on-stage situation, barking out both songs and orders with his usual characteristic gruffness.

The set he performed on those nights featured songs which were in many different ways part and

parcel of Feelgood history. There was a Nick Lowe tune ('Heart Of The City'), the Tyla Gang's 'Styrofoam', Gypie Mayo's 'Milk And Alcohol' and, of course, the ubiquitous Mickey Jupp's 'Down At The Doctors'. Most poignantly and significantly was a new cover in the Feelgood list: 'Road Runner', the Holland-Dozier-Holland classic which Lee had specifically requested they play. The song's lyrics, which feature the immortal lines 'I live the life I love and I love the life I live', could it seemed have been Lee Brilleaux's CV.

After each of the gigs as Lee came off the stage, Cousin Gary's heavyweight talents weren't needed: for a brief moment, it seemed that the shot of rhythm and blues had visibly picked Lee up as he animatedly mixed with his friends and fans alike. The Feelgoods had once again improbably 'played the live card' and come out of it with as exciting an LP as ever. Already enthusiastic conversations were

occurring with Nigel Kerr, the band's long-time agent, which were looking ahead to the summer with suggestions of Dr Feelgood maybe taking on a few festival dates when Lee felt stronger.

However it was not to be. Lee's illness was active again and another round of painful chemotherapy was on the cards. Kevin Morris recalls going round to the Proceeds to see how Lee was. 'He told me he had to go into hospital again. I said do you want to? He said "No". I said don't then. We just looked at each other and there was nothing to say. I knew he wasn't going to put himself through that ordeal again and that there could only be one consequence.'

In a very short time, Lee's strength failed dramatically and he chose to remain at home, nursed around the clock by SCENT – the Southend Community Extended Nursing Team, whose remit is to take care of terminally-ill patients

in their last days in the familiarity and comfort of their own home. So it was that on the 7 April 1994 Lee Brilleaux died, attended by his wife Shirley and their two children, Nicholas and Kelly, in the familiar surroundings of the Proceeds, Leigh-on-Sea. He was 41 years old and the big adventure that Lee had embraced with open arms was suddenly over.

By the weekend, every national newspaper in the UK was running a short piece announcing Lee's death which was soon followed by laudatory obituaries in *The Guardian*, *The Independent*, *The Times* and Lee's own favourite, *The Daily Telegraph*, which had said 'Bluff, cheery and hard-drinking to the last...Lee Brilleaux was a credit both to Essex Man and to the venerable traditions of British R&B'. *The Guardian* headlined theirs with a terse 'Life off the road' and a live stage shot of Lee captioned 'Lee Brilleaux, a fixture on the world's circuit.' It was all true.

The funeral, held on 15 April at St Clements Church in Leigh-on-Sea, was attended by Lee's wife and children along with the many family and friends that Lee had including, of course, all Dr Feelgood band members past and present. Kevin Morris organised the soundtrack, which featured

imagined that our friendship would grow and survive the pressures of the rock'n'roll life over the next 30 years. The artist-manager relationship is often portrayed as a precarious one, but Lee as my business partner never once allowed business decisions to impair our loyal friendship.

'His unique musical talent and gift for communication made him popular in every country in which we toured and although his stage persona was very different from the real Lee he was still as charismatic off-stage as on. His warm and generous personality earned him great respect and admiration. He had concern and consideration for all men and women, regardless of their position in life, and as most of you here know, his remarkable intelligence and fearlessly dry wit were already legendary. In the world of showbusiness, there are few who can pursue their career and still remain "one of the lads" down at the local pub, but Lee was able to do that because he always made sure that the artist's ego never over took the real person, the real Lee.

'With his impeccable manners and immaculate dress sense he was always interested in pursuing the lifestyle of the English gentlemen, rather than being seen as a showbiz celebrity. Lee was a hard-working, hard-drinking man who packed so much into each day of his life that he was often hard to keep up with – and in remembering this it is the only recompense for Lee's untimely death. He really did put more into his life than most people who live to be 100, and I can honestly say that it is the greatest privilege of my life to have known him...'

After the service, there followed a simple ceremony for immediate family and friends at Southend crematorium before the funeral party repaired to the Feelgood Music Bar for the wake. Beer flowed, instruments were strummed but, without the guv'nor in attendance, none of it seemed real.

two tracks Lee particularly enjoyed – Boccherini's 'Guitar Quintet', which featured a castanet section at the end which had always amused him, and his unofficial theme song 'Road Runner' as performed by Junior Walker.

It was here that his oldest friend and business manager Chris Fenwick delivered the following eulogy which Chris's wife, Beverley, had penned for the distraught pal to read to all present.

'As the manager of Dr Feelgood, I am lucky enough to say that Lee Brilleaux was my best friend. When we met at the age of 11 as playmates on the Canvey Marshes, we could never have

ONE STEP FORWARD

16

After Lee's death Chris found himself, for the first time since his teens, not only without his best mate to chivvy along but also without a band to run. All sorts of people in the business were soon all asking the same repetitive questions: 'Was the band going to continue in some form?' and 'What are you going to do next?' Lee's death had understandably knocked him for six and he wanted time away from it all to consider what was the best way forward. In reply to such questions: all the dazed Fenwick could say was 'I'm finished at the moment.'

Yet much as he wanted to lock the office door and shut up shop, the phones were constantly ringing and the fax machine was spewing out paper. All over Europe, bands and promoters who had worked with the band over the years were seeking permission to stage all manner of special tribute gigs. It would have been churlish to refuse and so Fenwick gave his blessing for several one-off shows to be staged at various venues across Europe featuring the name of the band and the familiar logo.

He turned up at these events to be greeted like a long-lost friend. Everyone, it seemed – fans, musicians and promoters alike – all wanted to say one last 'Cheers' in the common language they shared, rock'n'roll. Chris made only one stipulation, which was that any money raised at these events was to go straight to SCENT, the hospice charity that had nursed Lee in his final days at home.

Back home again, the office phones and faxes were still ringing hot – this time bringing news of a more alarming nature. In odd corners of England, America and Europe the Dr Feelgood name was it seemed now regarded as being 'up for grabs'. Posters had already been spotted by vigilant friends of the band advertising the Sounds of Dr Feelgood and the Feelgood Factors. Best of all was news of some American gunslinger who was about to get on a plane Stateside and come to England to front an outfit called Tribute to Dr Feelgood. Thanks...but no thanks.

Chris Fenwick in his office and in his element, 1997.

109

Anyone who's seen the hard-boiled gangster film *The Long Good Friday*, with Bob Hoskins cast as the villain, will remember the scene when certain characters unfortunate enough to have crossed him are wheeled into Nine Elms meat storage plant upside-down on meat hooks. It's an image which goes some way towards conjuring up Fenwick's mood at the time. Chris, however, prefers to employ 'blokes in cloaks' for such legal argy-bargy.

Chris sat down, picked up the phone and started putting the word out through his network of agents and other contacts across Europe and the UK that all bets were off: anyone who wanted to play ball with the Feelgood name was going to have to bat with him. As Chris says of these days: 'I thought no, I haven't worked all these years to just give it all away.' The ersatz posters came down, and for the first time in the history of Dr Feelgood there was no datesheet sitting on Fenwick's desk waiting to be filled in. It really was over.

There was still the sound of music in the air though, as on 10 May, which would have been Lee's 42nd birthday, the first of what was to be an annual event took place – the Lee Brilleaux Memorial Concert. Held at the Feelgood Music Bar, everyone who was anyone in the local music scene – along with those who counted Lee as a friend – gathered to play a tribute gig together. In attendance were the Inmates, Nine Below Zero, Eddie and the Hot Rods and – most poignantly of all – a Dr Feelgood line-up of Wilko, Sparko and Figure playing together for the first time in many years.

To coincide with this event, the live record of Lee's last gig entitled 'Down At The Doctors' was released. It was the perfect tribute. Shortly after this, in early July, the Dr Feelgood Music Bar finally closed its doors and the bulldozers moved in. Chris settled down to spend the rest of the year taking care of the inevitable business affairs a death brings. He had, in addition that July, one last service to perform.

Though Lee's body had been cremated as had been the family wish, his ashes had not as yet been taken care of. Chris and friends accordingly organised one last ceremony at which they could formally say goodbye in the best way they knew how. While they lined the Sea Wall at Canvey, a small boat chugged up along the Estuary and quietly cast Lee's ashes into the sea, close by the sandbank of Long Horse Island where he'd played pirates all those years ago. Now, with the ebb and flow of the tide, he was truly down by the jetty and forever a part of Canvey Island.

Next came a valedictory box set of Dr Feelgood music which Tim Chacksfield at EMI had cleared the way to produce. Broadcaster Stephen Foster on whose blues programme Lee had often appeared, was given the task of compiling a definitive 104-track compilation which was to draw a line under Lee's recording career.

There was also the day-to-day administration and management of Grand Records to organise. Chris, along with his assistant Ann Adley, had CD orders to be boxed up and shipped out across Europe, along with all the necessary paperwork. As the year-end approached, thoughts began about a possible future for the band and the idea of putting them back on the road...which had been Lee's final wish.

After a proper year had elapsed since Lee's demise, Chris Fenwick slowly started to pick up the pieces and move one step forward.

ON THE ROAD AGAIN

17

In the period immediately after Lee's death no-one from the final Feelgoods line-up had remotely considered the possibility of ever playing together again other than in the context of an annual memorial gig. It was, as Kevin and Steve both say, 'unthinkable'. However much a cliché, time really *is* a great healer and in the ensuing months many people who loved the band, fans and promoters alike, started to ask the same question – 'Are you getting a new singer in?'

Slowly the idea developed that perhaps what had once seemed to be the unthinkable was at least worth investigating. Chris placed the ball firmly in Kevin's court. Still too upset to piece it all together himself, he gave the project his blessing by telling the drummer: 'See if you can find someone…but leave me out of it.'

As Kevin embarked on this painstaking process, he recalled a prophetic 'on the road' conversation which he had had with Lee some years before, for no particular reason, in which Lee explicitly said: 'if anything happens to me speak to Wilko.' It was as if, despite all their differences, Lee still regarded the guitarist as a custodian of the Feelgood flame. With this in mind, Kevin spoke to Wilko in general terms about the project, but he was firmly established in his own successful solo career. Other considerations involved Sparko and Figure, who were occasionally going out as the Practice with Gypie Mayo and playing a few one-off gigs.

Finally, though, the thought was emerging that if anyone should give it a go then it should be the nucleus of the last official line-up. Kevin spoke to Steve Walwyn about the proposal, and two things convinced him it was right to consider going on. 'I think Lee would have liked it, and also I think a genuine fan would prefer to have a band playing Feelgood songs as opposed to nothing.'

Phil Mitchell was similarly contacted about a return to the fold. In the intervening years, he had become more settled at home and had built himself a recording and rehearsal studio and was itching to get back on the road with a band. Apart from anything else, there was an overiding feeling among the trio that, if they let the band fold, then the Dr Feelgood catalogue of songs they all enjoyed playing would effectively go with it.

Everyone was up for it, but still the spectre of finding a 'replacement' for Lee was hanging over them. It seemed like an impossible task. Several performers who had been suggested were tried out in the rehearsal studio. Some were straight

The line-up that put the Feelgoods back in business.

111

down the line singers, others singer-guitarists. Whoever they tried and no matter how good they were it just didn't feel right. The overall effect was always a change in the whole sound and vibe of the band. They needed someone who had the right credentials who wasn't going to 'impersonate' Lee – yet would still front the band in a recognisable way. As Phil put it, 'Some of the singers, although good, just made us sound like a covers band.'

With the word out on the street, a new name cropped up through a mutual friend of Kevin Morris. The singer's name was Pete Gage, a charismatic blues singer who'd been working the semi-pro circuit for several years. Gage had a lineage that stretched back into the early 1960s when he was 'a serious mod' popping pills on a Saturday night and going down to the Flamingo club in Soho every weekend where he'd combine an interest in the music of Georgie Fame or Zoot Money with the more pressing problem of pulling a bird. When he wasn't down the Flamingo, Pete was also a regular at places like the Crawdaddy, the Marquee and Eel Pie Island where the Rolling Stones, the Yardbirds and the Animals were going through their paces.

Pete's big break had come in 1966, when a band he was singing in had supported Jimi Hendrix at a gig in London's East End. In the audience that night was legendary bassist Jet Harris, formerly of the Shadows, who was putting a band together. He liked the sound of Pete's voice, and so it was that Pete found himself recording a Reg Presley original for the Fontana label called 'My Lady'. Harris's group had something of a jazzy feel to it, a touch of Booker T and the MGs mixed with a dash of Howard Tate. As Pete now says of those heady, formative days 'I wore a suit back then, Jet was very showbiz-minded. I was 20 and having a ball.'

The band wasn't to prove to be a long-term affair and Pete eventually returned to the semi-pro circuit while he trained formally to become a psychiatric nurse and eventually moved to Bristol. He still kept in touch with the music scene over the years, playing both solo and in all manner of impromptu bands. By the time he received a call from Kevin Morris in 1995, he had taken voluntary redundancy from the National Health Service and was pushing himself forward once again on the pub circuit down in the west country.

Though he'd never seen them live, he had heard of Dr Feelgood and the phonecall came as something of a shock. Kevin invited Pete down to Canvey for an audition and asked him to prepare a setlist of nine songs. Determined to demonstrate his abilities, Pete sat down and started to learn the songs 'parrot-fashion' so he was able to perform them confidently without the use of lyric sheets.

Phil Mitchell, recalling that first audition, says that 'When we played "Back In The Night" it suddenly sounded like us again. Pete really stood

out.' Additionally, as Pete was older than the other auditionees, he lent the proceedings a certain gravitas it was felt a young gunslinger simply couldn't muster. However enthusiastic they were Kevin, Phil and Steve made no snap decisions. Pete was certainly looking good, but they had to be positive they were making the right choice. After all, to go back up onstage as Dr Feelgood and get it wrong would be a disaster.

A two-month decision-making period followed, during which time other singers were still in the frame. Pete was eventually asked to lay down a track with the band to see how his voice recorded. He even had his picture taken with the band to see how that looked. Everything that could be tested out was. Slowly things were beginning to slot into place.

By the summer of 1995, Pete Gage was ready to be confirmed as the new singer and frontman of Dr Feelgood. In order to ease Pete into the band, a few low-key UK dates were slotted in followed by a short hop over to Europe. Phil: 'We had no intention of ever getting a Brilleaux clone in. We said to Pete do your own thing, sing the songs your way.' Which is exactly what Pete did.

Nevertheless, there were some remarkable coincidences. Pete had purchased himself a stage

suit from the same theatrical costumiers in Soho that Lee used to frequent – and, unbeknown to him, had it cut from the same material as Lee had once chosen. Onstage, with sweat spreading across the back of his jacket, the band momentarily felt the distinct presence of Lee as they breathed life once again into some classic Feelgood tracks.

Pete, however, wasn't simply slotting in and just occupying someone else's shoes. He was very much his own man – an experienced singer with his own distinctive 'shovel of gravel' voice and the ability to project himself and the band in a way that was different from the past yet still retained the hallmarks of what Dr Feelgood were all about. In addition, as Pete had never seen or met Brilleaux, he was incapable of being either being directly intimidated by the stature of the man he had been asked to follow onto the stage or of being lured into some impressionistic routine. As Phil puts it: 'He became the new frontman in a very genuine way.'

To consolidate the new line-up and press a new footprint into the cement, the band decided to record a new studio album, collecting together a selection of suitable covers spiced up with some originals from Steve Walwyn and Dave Bronze. The backing tracks laid down in a few, very cut-and-dried live sessions at Phil Mitchell's studio were then taken along to Dave Bronze's home studio where he worked in a more intensive manner with Pete Gage to record the vocals, spending some considerable time to ensure that they were right.

Tracks such as Peter Green's 'World Keeps Turning', which would have seemed out of place before, were deliberately picked as they suited Pete's bluesier voice and the number duly established itself as a live feature of the new act. The resulting album was given the title 'On The Road Again' (at Beverley Fenwick's suggestion) not only after the Canned Heat song but to mark the band's full-time return to the gigging circuit.

Chris Fenwick had reaffirmed contacts with agents across Europe and dates were gradually being slotted in once again. In May 1996, the Third Memorial Concert at the Grand saw Pete Gage formally introduced to the Feelgood cognoscenti and another bridge in the transitional process had been crossed. Dr Feelgood were back on the road.

KING FOR A DAY

In his erudite review of this book when it was published first time round, former *NME* kingpin and all-round good guy Charles Shaar Murray attempted to come to grips with the various comings and goings that the outfit known as Dr Feelgood had experienced over the years by condensing down the big picture into a pocket-sized biog...

'Then the one who played the music fucked off...the band started to do even better...then he retired and someone else stepped into his shoes, after a while the originals left as well, that left the one in the middle and the one backstage...he went off on his holidays...' And so on. You have to admit that to an outsider, let alone a real twenty-carat groover like Chuck Murray, these comings and goings do seem somewhat perplexing.

Remember the old chestnut about 'my grandfather's axe'? No? It's a question Feelgood fans have had to grapple with on more than one occasion over the past thirty years. It goes something like this. My father inherited my grandfather's axe and in time replaced the rotting handle. Eventually I, too, inherited the axe, and soon replaced the rusting blade. Thus the philosophical question: is it still my grandfather's axe? Well, yes and no and, equally, bollocks. Seeking an answer to this question in the context of the Feelgoods is a tedious and pointless pursuit.

It's a question present guitarist Steve Walwyn recalls asking himself years ago when he clocked the cover of the *NME* and its blood-chilling headline which announced that Wilko Johnson had quit the band. As Steve reflects, 'Even now, when I think of Dr Feelgood, I think of Wilko and Lee on the cover of 'Stupidity'. But then there are an awful lot of people out there who never saw that band; they're familiar with more recent line-ups, particularly the present one.'

Talking to the band today, it is clear that, from time to time, they have to deal with fans and music-biz merchants who simply can't take the upheaval in their stride. Some have even been known to offer the cold shoulder as a new inmate runs onto the field of play. But as the ever-stoical Phil

Mitchell puts it, 'We have our detractors, of course, but you can't please everyone all the time. At the end of the day we have to please ourselves and say if you don't like what we are up to then don't come to the gig.'

The last word on this goes to skinsman and bandleader Kevin Morris: 'Of course I understand when people say that Dr Feelgood begins and ends with the original band, but I have to override that because I also know that an awful lot of people like Dr Feelgood, the songs we play and the way in which we play them. They come along for the moment. We want to do it and we enjoy doing it. Time has moved on since Lee passed away. When that happened the whole idea of the band was unthinkable, then it gradually became thinkable, and then it became practical. These things happen…'

So let's finally put that tired old axe back in the woodshed where it belongs and pick up another far more potent weapon – namely a battered Fender Telecaster – and hit the low down and dirty opening chords to John Lee Hooker's 'Mad Man Blues'. 'I came home last night about nine o'clock…I got the mad man blues, mad man blues…'

The sound of this persistent boogie, emanating from a fifty-watt speaker cab and featuring Steve Walwyn on solo swamp guitar, is like a spike cutting into a block of ice. Up front Robert Kane, gives the audience another tickle: '…Mad Man Blues!' Before long, they are joined by the rump a'thump rhythm section of Morris and Mitchell who rip into the number like ram-raiders doing a high-street store at Christmas. (By the way, the audience are as usual going mental.)

Decked out in a black frock coat with matching shirt and shades, Robert Kane is the new frontman of the band. With something approaching five hundred Feelgood gigs under his belt already, the term 'fresh fish' seems totally inappropriate. He is not the fairground barker that Brilleaux was, nor the Rod the Mod shovel of gravel that was Pete Gage. This is both a gear shift and also a tyre change. Equally captivating as the past yet palpably different and very, very effective.

Robert has been a professional singer for some years, and was well into a six-year stretch with the Animals when Kevin donned his poacher's jacket and approached him with an offer he couldn't refuse. Phil characterises his persona as being '…more in the pop idiom. He enjoys performing on stage and his presence has really modernised and revitalised the group.'

And so he has. The upfront presentation is a world away from the packet of twenty, non-tipped, fist-punching delivery that was the Brilleaux hallmark. It feels that, at last, the towering presence of Lee Brilleaux has been deftly and respectfully laid to rest (although never forgotten) in favour of a newer, more eclectic approach which is having the satisfactory effect of introducing the band to a wider younger audience while, at the same time, keeping older fans happy.

As Robert puts it: 'When I joined the band, I said to people I am the singer now. I'm not a Lee Brilleaux, I have my own way of singing and performing and that's how I'm going to play it…' The familiar and consistent back line of Walwyn, Mitchell and Morris, of course, smash away at their respective instruments with the same ferocity and attack as ever – only now it seems a more subtle personality is enticing the audience out of their respective shells and onto the dance floor. Like they say, a change is as good as a rest. So why the change?

Immediately after the decision to put the Feelgoods back together had been made, semi-pro singer Pete Gage was charged with the seemingly impossible (and frankly unenviable) job of fronting a band whose singer was variously 'on stage a law unto himself.' (Mitchell) and 'a man responsible for much of the high jinx as well as the clarity of the band.' (Morris) For the rest of us he was simply 'the Gaffer'.

Gage grabbed hold of the empty mic spot with enthusiasm and a new urgency swept through the band. It was an odd one at first for all concerned, both on and off stage, but the boys were back in action. Gagey might have decked himself out in a stage suit cut by Brilleaux's own tailor in Brewer St but he was nevertheless his own man. Pete Gage fronted the band with aplomb and helped steer it through the new situation. It worked. In spades.

However, being in a band is never just simply about what goes on on stage. Touring at the Feelgood level of two hundred-plus shows a year is serious graft which, however comfortable you make it with a glass or two of good wine, an à la carte menu and a good hotel, still entails being in close proximity with the same people 24/7. Much of it is spent in the restrictive confines of 'the small bottle' (Mitchell), in other words the tour bus.

Being in a band is often likened to a marriage. There will be tensions from time to time, plates will get smashed, dinners scraped into the bin…remember the Fenwick troublemaker flag? Suffice to say that the reconstituted team were slowly discovering each other and, day by day, it was becoming clear that this marriage was never going to go diamond. It was therefore mutually agreed that Pete was to stand down. While these issues were rising to the surface, Kevin had already clocked Robert out on the circuit in Europe. When the time was right he made his move and yet another chapter in the Feelgood

Robert Kane exchanged life as an Animal for a Feelgood stint.

biography was opened up.

It was a decision Morris remains very happy about. 'Right from the off, Robert had a very independent air. It was clear he wasn't going to simply absorb himself into some established footprint of what a Dr Feelgood frontman does…I think we have gathered a lot of strength from this approach.' Perhaps the decision to make these changes and to seek a new frontman can be best expressed by the old adage which Kevin often refers to as the 'Brillometer'. What would Lee have done in a similar situation? Does it feel right? If not, why not? Every home should have one.

The Feelgood organisation is a seasonal thing. Like migrating birds, they find themselves in familiar haunts at particular times of the year. I catch up with them in Zurich for a bit of a jolly-up. The gig tonight is an old converted cinema, the audience a typical Friday-night crowd who are simply, like most of the rest of Europe, up for a good night out, with a few beers and perhaps a promise on the side. The Feelgoods have no problem delivering that prescription.

The set is a broad-based plan of action. Old beat favourites like 'Roxette', 'She Does It Right' and 'All Through The City' sit effortlessly next to broader Chicago Chess catalogue numbers like 'The Walk' and 'Help Me' – not to mention a startlingly fresh

version of Chuck Berry's 'Nadine' which opens the set and establishes the requisite moodiness from the off.

It goes without saying that the band execute all of these songs with their usual snap, crackle and pop. The name Steve Walwyn has to be picked out here in big neon letters. Any three-piece needs a guitarist who can hold it all together without leaving huge gaps behind to fill in. Walwyn is that man. Self-effacing and calm off stage, he becomes on stage a man with the St Vitus' dance. Possessed with a thousand-yard stare, he doesn't so much play his Telecaster…rather he chokes it like it was a Thanksgiving chicken.

His blues-playing is up there with Clapton, Stevie Ray Vaughan and the late, great Rory Gallagher. 'Down By The Jetty Blues' and 'Mad Man Blues' have, in particular, become blistering showcases for his string-bending talents. He can boogie on down like John Lee Hooker, get dirty like a Fab Thunderbird or simply let rip with a glorious flourish of notes à la Clapton. Then a swift gear change and he becomes the snapping rhythm king with decisive Steve Cropper-like chops.

Every king needs a court, and knights errant Kevin Morris and Phil Mitchell deceptively supply the necessary backbeat – uncomplicated, rocksteady drum and bass. Robert Kane is simply something of a revelation. A completely different performer in every way to a Brilleaux. Decked out in a black frock coat and matching shades, he stalks the stage like a Southern bible-belt preacher. Tonight he's preaching the gospel of Canvey Island with a microphone in one hand and a harmonica in the other.

He has a considered way of singing which means that you can hear all the words: he doesn't spit them out, rather he eases them out and savours them like the pearls they are. His easygoing yet forthright presence has changed the band for certain. They remain rough and ready, still a bit gruff around the gills but also accessible and, most importantly, forward-looking.

Tonight in Zurich Robert has to work that bit harder to persuade an non-partisan audience to let their hair down. After a little polite goading, the first few dissenters break free and take to the front of the dance floor, soon followed by the rest of the pack. By this time the band are laying down the opening riff to 'Down By The Jetty Blues' it is impossible to resist as the whole club starts to respond in a series of physical jerks and handclaps. The reception is warm, generous and passionate.

Nevertheless, the après-gig mood in the dressing room is lacklustre. The band feel a little low on energy. Robert, in particular, never felt he connected. As a performer he needs that empathy with the audience. Tonight, although the gig was a

cracker, the consensus was that it was a good one but not as good as it gets. Close but no cigar.

The following day, the white van crosses Switzerland heading for the medieval town of Bern. On a brief shopping spree into town it becomes clear that Orson Welles was probably right in his quip about the Swiss and Cuckoo clocks (seemingly everywhere), not to mention bears in pits and statues of gargantuan oafs biting babies' heads off.

To add to the prevailing atmosphere of eccentricity our neat-looking hotel is a late-1970s tower block over looking the town. The decor is essentially white leatherette with silver disco light fittings. Think of a cross between the interior decor of *2001 – A Space Odyssey* and *A Clockwork Orange* and you'll get the picture.

The gig tonight is even more outré. Located on the outskirts of the city in a tranquil and frighteningly manicured countryside location is a four storey wooden chalet-type affair. The owner is a somewhat eccentric inveterate rock'n'roller who has over the years amassed a huge collection of junk – old fairground machines, metal sculptures, skeletons and a myriad of stuffed animals and transformed this wooden building and the grounds surrounding it into a temple of barminess.

The grounds are packed full of odd home-made sculptures that wouldn't seem out of place on Scrapyard Challenge. In the front garden sits a

huge stone carving of Bart Simpson astride a trickling water fountain. Beyond the metal gates is a huge wooden ball with a door in it. Inside the actual gaff is another world. This is like Barney's Beanery – the Keinholtz sculpture of the bar of the same name that you can walk right into in and sit alongside drinkers who have giant clocks for heads.

Ever seen a pike looking at you with a pair of cheap 1970s headphones on? What about a flying pig over the stage? Did I mention the army of metal ants or the demented animatronic squirrel? You get the picture. In short, the perfect emporium for a bit of lowdown rock'n'roll. By nine o'clock, the compact club is literally heaving with Swiss rockers. The small stage juts out into the centre of the building. Look up from the front mic spot and you'll see three or four tiers gaping back down at you.

The words 'eating' 'out of' and 'hand ' come to mind as the band methodically rip the place apart. Tonight there is no 'nice

to meet you warm up', no reticence to come forward. In fact, from the back it is hard to see where the band starts and the audience ends. It is a simple whites of the eyes gig. Pure, highly-charged rock'n'roll.

Once again, Steve Walwyn leaves an indelible imprint on peoples' minds. During the climax to one number he finds himself out of control, lurching right off the front of the stage and into the middle of an ecstatic audience. Not to be outdone, Phil stands on his amplifier and rocks it back and forward. Kane slaps his hands and Morris slams his bass pedal to the floor. I am transported back to the early days in London's Dingwalls as we end with a shot of 'Tequila' and a splash of 'Bonie Moronie', a few cubes of 'Route 66' being thrown in for good measure. A perfect cocktail to end a perfect three-encore set.

After this bravura performance I stroll backstage where a still ecstatic Kevin Morris virtually grabs me by the lapels and

points back at the scene of the crime while wiping the sweat off his face. 'You see! That's what it's all about! That's what it's all about! That moment…' As Brilleaux once put it, 'It's a high…but you're definitely hurting yourself.'

21ST-CENTURY CANVEY

The Feelgood camp still inevitably gravitates around the Thames estuary. The firm may not live on Canvey Island itself but nevertheless it remains their spiritual homeland. The office is still there, reassuringly located above a bookies'. One of the most important dates in the calendar is the Lee Brilleaux Anniversary gig, held annually at the Oyster Fleet Hotel. Built on the site of the old Feelgood Music Bar, this is a mid-range hotel aimed at wedding parties, travelling reps and salesmen.

A blue plaque on the wall outside reminds passers-by that a bloke named Brilleaux once tested the stage, not to mention the counter, on the very ground they are standing on in 1994. Around this parish the memory of Lee Brilleaux just won't lie down. It's not a morbid thing, it's called enough respect.

Kevin: 'I think about him almost every day; he was a very powerful character, intelligent, articulate. A pretty exceptional person.' Singer Robert Kane recalls flicking through the *NME* of 1976 and seeing the battered, iconic white suit hanging up against a dressing-room wall. (Caption: Sleeve of the Year) It was to him then and remains today the perfect rock'n'roll image.

Every year Feelgoods past and present along with buddy, buddy friends like ace tunesmith Larry Wallis and sometime bass-player/producer Dave Bronze hit the stage, give it a lash and remember the past. I ask Chris Fenwick how he regards

things now. After so, so many ups and downs, does he feel bulletproof? 'I never think that! That's a very dangerous thing for a manager to think. Things go wrong, shit happens. It's much better to just take log of the past. When Lee died it was like a crash-landing, but we've taken off again and we're gaining altitude. I deal in reality sandwiches, not how things should be but how they are…'

An important part of the anniversary day is Chris's increasingly popular Brilleaux walk, a stroll around Canvey Island taking in the various sights: the Lobster Smack, the Labworth Cafe, the location where 'Down By The Jetty' was photographed and the house where Lee grew up. Oil City lies off to the north with the Thames, where Lee's ashes were finally scattered, meandering out into the North Sea. Like they say, if you seek his monument look around you.

It is now time to leave the eulogies alone. The Feelgoods have come through all the trials and tribulations to become something larger than just a band. They are a community, an extended family. They mean a lot to a lot of people, no matter at what point in their evolution they picked up on the story.

The band will continue to entertain people around the world with their very English take on the musical genre of blues and R&B. Be it the UK, Europe, Japan or Russia, they speak an international language that anyone who has ever combed their hair into a quiff, sported a over-ripe Kaftan or strummed a tennis racket in their adolescent bedroom understands. The world is certainly a better place with the Feelgoods in it.

Remember that old axe I mentioned earlier? Take it from me. It still cuts wood, and then some. I'd watch my step with it if I were you.

DR FEELGOOD DISCOGRAPHY

SINGLES
(All in picture sleeves except *)

Roxette/(Get Your Kicks On) Route 66*
United Artists 7" UP 35760.
Released November 1974.

She Does It Right/I Don't Mind*
United Artists 7" UP 35815.
Released March 1975.

Back In The Night/I'm A Man*
United Artists 7" UP 35857.
Released July 1975.

Roxette (Live)/Keep It Out Of Sight (Live)*
United Artists 7" UP 36171.
Released October 1976.

Sneakin' Suspicion/Lights Out*
United Artists 7" UP 36255.
Released May 1977.

She's A Wind Up/Hi-Rise
United Artists 7" UP 36304.
Released September 1977.

She's A Wind Up/Hi-Rise/Homework (Live)*
United Artists 12" 12 UP 36304.
Released September 1977.

Baby Jane/Looking Back
United Artists 7" UP 36332.
Released November 1977.

Baby Jane/Looking Back/You Upset Me Baby (Live)
United Artists 12" 12 UP 36332.
Released November 1977.

Down At The Doctors/Take A Tip
United Artists 7" UP 36444.
Released September 1978.

Milk And Alcohol/Every Kind Of Vice
United Artists 7" UP 36468.
Released January 1979. (Available in black, brown and white vinyl with matching PS)

As Long As The Price Is Right/Down At The (Other) Doctors
United Artists black vinyl 7" UP 36506, blue vinyl 7" XUP 3650, brown vinyl 7" YUP 36506, violet vinyl 7" ZUP 36506.
Released April 1979.

It Don't Take But A Few Minutes/Blues Jam
United Artists 7" UP 36514.
Released 1979.
(Not strictly a Feelgood single but produced by Sparko, featuring Lew Lewis and released under the alias of the Oil City Sheiks.)

Put Him Out Of Your Mind/Bend Your Ear
United Artists 7" BP 306.
Released October 1979.

Hong Kong Money/Keeka Smeeka
United Artists 7" BP 338.
Released February 1980.

No Mo Do Yakamo/Best In The World
United Artists 7" BP 366.
Released September 1980.

Jumping From Love To Love/Love Hound
United Artists 7" BP 374.
Released November 1980.

Violent Love/A Case Of The Shakes
United Artists 7" BP 386.
Released January 1981.

Waiting For Saturday Night/Eileen
Liberty 7" BP 404.
Released October 1981.

Trying To Live My Life Without You/Murder In The First Degree
Chiswick 7" DICE 16.
Released September 1982.

Crazy About Girls/Something Out Of Nothing
Chiswick 7" DICE 18.
Released March 1983.

Dangerous/Can't Find The Lady
Demon 7" D1030.
Released September 1984.

My Way/She's In The Middle*
Demon 7" D 1032.
Released December 1984.

Don't Wait Up/Something Good
Stiff 7" BUY 253.
Released August 1986.
(Initially issued shrink-wrapped with free single:
Back In The Night/Milk And Alcohol* Stiff 7"
FBUY 253).

Don't Wait Up/Something Good/Rockin' With Somebody New
Stiff 12" BUY IT 253.
Released August 1986.

See You Later Alligator/I Love You So You're Mine
Stiff 7" BUY 255.
Released November 1986.

See You Later Alligator/I Love You So You're Mine/What Do You Think Of That
Stiff 12" BUY IT 255.
Released November 1986.

Hunting Shooting Fishing/Big Enough
Stiff 7" BUY 259.
Released June 1987.

Hunting Shooting Fishing/Big Enough/Don't Underestimate Your Enemy
Stiff 12" BUY IT 259.
Released June 1987.

Crash Your Car Megamix
Stiff Cassette Single Crash 1.
Released June 1987. (Consists of extended
'megamix' of Dr Feelgood tracks including
'Hunting Shooting Fishing'.)

Milk And Alcohol (New Recipe)/She's Got Her Eyes On You
EMI 7" EM 89.
Released April 1989.

Milk And Alcohol (New Recipe)/She's Got Her Eyes On You/Mad Man Blues
EMI 12" 12 EM 89.
Released April 1989.

ALBUMS

Down By The Jetty
United Artists UAS 29727.
Released January 1975 (reissued as Edsel ED160 in 1987 and as GRAND 05 in January 1990).
She Does It Right – Boom Boom – The More I Give – Roxette – One Weekend – That Ain't The Way To Behave – I Don't Mind – Twenty Yards Behind – Keep It Out Of Sight – All Through The City – Cheque Book – Oyeh – Bonie Moronie/Tequila

Malpractice
United Artists UAS 29880.
Released October 1975 (reissued as GRAND 09 in August 1990).
I Can Tell – Going Back Home – Back In The Night – Another Man – Rolling And Tumbling – Don't Let Your Daddy Know – Watch Your Step – Don't You Just Know It – Riot In Cell Block No 9 – Because You're Mine – You Shouldn't Call The Doctor (If You Can't Afford The Bills)

Stupidity
United Artists UAS 29990.
Released September 1976. (Initially issued with free live 7": Riot In Cell Block No 9/Johnny Be Goode* United Artists 7" FEEL 1.)
Talking About You – Twenty Yards Behind – Stupidity – All Through The City – I'm A Man – Walking The Dog – She Does It Right – Going Back Home – I Don't Mind – Back In The Night – I'm A Hog For You Baby – Checking Up On My Baby – Roxette

Sneakin' Suspicion
United Artists UAS 30075.
Released May 1977 (reissued as GRAND 13 in September 1991).
Sneakin' Suspicion – Paradise – Nothin' Shakin' (But The Leaves On The Trees) – Time And The Devil – Lights Out – Lucky Seven – All My Love – You'll Be Mine – Walking On The Edge – Hey Mama, Keep Your Big Mouth Shut

Be Seeing You
United Artists UAS 30123.
Released September 1977 (reissued as Edsel ED238 with different sleeve in 1987 and as GRAND14 in September 1991).
Ninety-Nine And A Half (Won't Do) – She's A Wind Up – I Thought I Had It Made – I Don't Wanna Know – That's It, I Quit – As Long As The Price Is Right – Hi-Rise – My Buddy Buddy Friends – Baby Jane – The Blues Had A Baby And They Named It Rock'n'Roll – Looking Back – 60 Minutes Of Your Love

Private Practice
United Artists UA 30184. Released September 1978 (reissued as GRAND 01 in October 1988).
Down At The Doctors – Every Kind Of Vice – Things Get Better – Milk And Alcohol – Night Time – Let's Have A Party – Take A Tip – It Wasn't Me – Greaseball – Sugar Shaker

As It Happens
United Artists UAK 30239.
Released June 1979 (reissued as GRAND 15 in September 1995). (Originally issued with free live 'Encore EP':- Riot In Cell Block No. 9/The Blues Had A Baby And They Named It Rock'n'Roll/Lights Out/Great Balls Of Fire United Artists 7" FEEL 2.)
Take A Tip – Every Kind Of Vice – Down At The Doctors – Baby Jane – Sugar Shaker – Things Get Better – She's A Wind Up – Ninety-Nine And A Half (Won't Do) – My Buddy Buddy Friends – Milk And Alcohol – Matchbox – As Long As The Price Is Right – Night Time

Let It Roll
United Artists UAG 30269.
Released September 1979 (reissued as GRAND 07 in October 1989).
Java Blue – Feels Good – Put Him Out Of Your Mind – Bend Your Ear – Hong Kong Money – Keeka Smeeka – Shotgun – Pretty Face – Riding On The L & N – Drop Everything And Run

A Case Of The Shakes
United Artists UAG 30311.
Released September 1980 (reissued as Edsel ED189 in 1987 and as GRAND 10 in August 1990).
Jumping From Love To Love – Going Some Place Else – Best In The World – Punch Drunk – King For A Day – Violent Love – No Mo Do Yakamo – Love Hound – Coming To You – Who's Winning – Drives Me Wild – A Case Of The Shakes

On The Job
Liberty LBG 30328.
Released August 1981 (reissued as GRAND 16 in September 1995).
Drives Me Wild – Java Blue – Jumping From Love To Love – Pretty Face – No Mo Do Yakamo – Love Hound – Best In The World – Who's Winning – Riding On The L & N – A Case Of The Shakes – Shotgun Blues – Goodnight Vienna

Casebook
Liberty LBG 30341.
Released November 1981.
Roxette – (Get Your Kicks On) Route 66 – She Does It Right – Riot In Cell Block No 9 – Back In The Night – You Shouldn't Call The Doctor – She's A Wind Up – Looking Back – Baby Jane – Milk And Alcohol – As Long As The Price Is Right – Down At The Doctors – Night Time – Put Him Out Of Your Mind – Hong Kong Money – Waiting For Saturday Night

Fast Women And Slow Horses
Chiswick TOSS 4.
Released October 1982 (reissued as GRAND 03 in May 1989).
She's The One – Monkey – Sweet Sweet Lovin' – Trying To Live My Life Without You – Rat Race – Baby Jump – Crazy About Girls – Sugar Bowl – Educated Fool – Bum's Rush – Baby Why Do You Treat Me This Way – Beautiful Delilah

Doctor's Orders
Demon FIEND 29.
Released October 1984 (reissued as GRAND 06 in January 1990).
Close But No Cigar – So Long – You Don't Love Me – My Way – Neighbour, Neighbour – Talk Of The Devil – Hit Git And Split – I Can't Be Satisfied – Saturday Night Fish Fry – Drivin' Wheel – It Ain't Right – I Don't Worry About A Thing – She's In The Middle – Dangerous

Mad Man Blues
ID 12" Mini-LP NOSE 5.
Released October 1985. (First mispressed with 'Don't Start Me Talking' instead of 'My Babe'.)
Dust My Broom – Dimples -Tore Down – Mad Man Blues – My Babe – Rock Me Baby

Mad Man Blues
French import LP Lolita 5042.
Released October 1985 (this version reissued as GRAND 02 in October 1988).
Dust My Broom – Something You Got – Dimples – Living On The Highway – Tore Down – Mad Man Blues – I've Got News For You – My Babe – Can't Find The Lady – Rock Me Baby

Brilleaux
Stiff SEEZ 65.
Released August 1986 (reissued as GRAND 04 in May 1989).
I Love You, So You're Mine – Big Enough – Don't Wait Up – Get Rhythm – Where Is The Next One? – Play Dirty – Grow Too Old – Rough Ride – I'm A Real Man – Come Over Here – Take What You Can Get

Case History – The Best Of Dr Feelgood
EMI CDP 7467112.
Released April 1987.
Going Back Home – Back In The Night – Roxette – She Does It Right – Sneakin' Suspicion – No Mo Do Yakamo – She's A Wind Up – As Long As The Price Is Right – Down At The Doctors – Milk And Alcohol – Violent Love – Jumping From Love To Love – Best In The World – Rat Race – Close But No Cigar – Play Dirty – Don't Wait Up – See You Later Alligator

Classic
Stiff SEEZ 67.
Released September 1987 (reissued as GRAND 11 in August 1990). (Reissue includes extra track 'Lights Of Downtown' and has different cover. Also commonly available as French import LP Off The Track OTT 10002 with alternate versions and track order.)
Hunting Shooting Fishing – Break These Chains – Heartbeat – (I Wanna) Make Love To You – Highway 61 – Quit While You're Behind – Nothing Like It – Spy Vs Spy – Hurricane – Crack Me Up – See You Later Alligator

Singles – The UA Years
Liberty EM 1332.
Released May 1989.
Roxette – She Does It Right – Back In The Night – Going Back Home – Riot In Cell Block No 9 – Sneakin' Suspicion – She's A Wind Up – Baby Jane – Down At The Doctors – Milk And Alcohol – As Long As The Price Is Right – Put Him Out Of Your Mind – Hong Kong Money – No Mo Do Yakamo – Jumping From Love To Love – Violent Love – Waiting For Saturday Night – Monkey – Trying To Live My Life Without You – Crazy About Girls – My Way – Mad Man Blues – Don't Wait Up – See You Later Alligator – Hunting Shooting Fishing

Live In London
Grand GRAND 08.
Released May 1990.
King For A Day – You Upset Me – As Long As The Price Is Right – Mad Man Blues – She Does It Right – Baby Jane – Quit While You're Behind – Back In The Night – Milk And Alcohol – See You Later Alligator – Down At The Doctors – Route 66 – Going Back Home – Bonie Moronie/Tequila

Stupidity Plus (Live 1976-1990)
Liberty EM 1388.
Released March 1991.
I'm Talking About You – Twenty Yards Behind – Stupidity – All Through The City – I'm A Man – Walking The Dog – She Does It Right – Going Back Home – I Don't Mind – Back In The Night – I'm A Hog For You – Checking Up On My Baby – Roxette – Riot In Cell Block No 9 – Johnny B Goode – Take A Tip – Every Kind Of Vice – She's A Wind Up – No Mo Do Yakamo – Love Hound – Shotgun Blues – King For A Day – Milk And Alcohol – Down At The Doctors

Primo
Grand GRAND 12.
Released June 1991.
Heart Of The City – My Sugar Turns To Alcohol – Going Down – No Time – World In A Jug – If My Baby Quit Me – Primo Blues – Standing At The Crossroads Again – Been Down So Long – Don't Worry Baby – Down By The Jetty (Blues) – Two Times Nine

The Feelgood Factor
Grand GRAND 17.
Released July 1993.
The Feelgood Factor – Tanqueray – Tell Me No Lies – Styrofoam – I'm In The Mood For You – Double Crossed – Lying About The Blues – She Moves Me – Wolfman Calling – One Step Forward – One To Ten – Fool For You

Down At The Doctors
Grand GRAND 018.
Released April 1994.
If My Baby Quit Me – Styrofoam – Tanqueray – Road Runner – Wolfman Callin' – Double Crossed – One Step Forward – Mojo Workin' – Milk And Alcohol – Down At The Doctors – Freddie's Footsteps – Heart Of The City

Looking Back

Liberty ACDFEEL 195.
Released October 1995.

On The Road Again

Grand GRAND 19.
Released August 1996.
Wine Women And Whisky – Sweet Louise – World Keeps Turning – On The Road Again – Instinct To Survive – Mellow Down Easy – Going Out West – Cheap At Half The Price – Second Opinion – What Am I To Believe – Repo Man – You Got Me

Twenty Five Years Of Dr Feelgood

Grand GRAND 20.
Released April 1997.
Compilation of released material

Centenary Collection

EMI 7243 8 59633 2 2
Released 1997
Compilation of released material

Stupidity

Grand GRAND 21
Released 1998
Track listing as previous

Live At The BBC 1974-75

Grand GRAND 22
Released 1999
My Baby, Your Baby – I'm Talking About You – One Weekend – Rock Me Baby – Bonie Moronie – She Does It Right – Twenty Yards Behind – The More I Give – Boom Boom – All Through The City – Talk To Me Baby – Route 66 – I Can Tell – Going Back Home – Don't You Just Know It – Roxette – Another Man – I Don't Mind – Riot In Cell Block No 9 – Rollin' And Tumblin' – You Shouldn't Call The Doctor (If You Can't Afford The Bills)

Chess Masters

Grand GRAND 23
Released May 2000
Nadine – Date Bait – You Gotta Help Me – Talkin' Bout You – The Walk – 29 Ways – Who Do You Love – If Walls Could Talk – Send For The Doctor – Killing Floor – Suzie Q – Don't Start Me Talking – Gimme One More Shot – Hoochie Coochie Man

Complete BBC Sessions 1973-1978

Grand GRAND 24
Released 2001
She Does It Right – I Don't Mind – Riot In Cell Block No 9 – Tore Down – Checking Up On My Baby (Rec 24.10.73) The More I Give – Boom Boom – All Through The City – Talk To Me Baby (Rec 13.11.74) I Don't Mind – I'm A Hog For You Baby – Keep It Out Of Sight – Route 66 (Rec 21.1.75) You Upset Me Baby – She's A Wind Up – Baby Jane – 99 And A Half (Rec 20.9.77) Night Time – Take A Tip – Down At The Doctors – Sugar Shaker (Rec 5.9.78)

Singled Out – UA/Liberty As, Bs & Rarities

EMI 534 242 2
Released 2001
3CD compilation of released material

Finely Tuned

Grand GRAND 25
Released October 2002
Wilko: She Does It Right – The More I Give – You Shouldn't Call The Doctor – Roxette – Going Back Home **Gypie:** I Don't Wanna Know – Down At The Doctors – Milk And Alcohol – Going Someplace Else – Best In The World **Johnny Guitar:** Sweet Sweet Lovin' – Beautiful Delilah – Murder In The First Degree – Something Out Of Nothing – Alimony (Unreleased) **Gordon:** You Don't Love Me – Mad Man Blues – Something Good – Hunting Shooting Fishing – Don't Underestimate Your Enemy **Steve:** Down By The Jetty Blues – Double Crossed – Solitary Blues – The Walk – You Gotta Help Me

Down At The BBC: In Concert 1977-78

Grand GRAND 26
Released October 2002
Looking Back – Stupidity – You'll Be Mine – You Upset Me Baby – Homework – Baby Jane – The Blues Had A Baby And They Named It Rock'n'Roll – That's It I Quit – Lucky Seven – She's A Wind Up – Lights Out – Looking Back – Sugar Shaker – I Thought I Had It Made – Ninety Nine And A Half – Milk & Alcohol – Night Time – Shotgun Blues – You Upset Me Baby – Down At The Doctors – She's A Wind Up – Lights Out